FOSTERING STATE-TRIBAL COLLABORATION

FOSTERING STATE-TRIBAL COLLABORATION

An Indian Law Primer

Andrea Wilkins

ROWMAN & LITTLEFIELD
Lanham • Boulder • New York • London

Published by Rowman & Littlefield
A wholly owned subsidiary of The Rowman & Littlefield Publishing Group, Inc.
4501 Forbes Boulevard, Suite 200, Lanham, Maryland 20706
www.rowman.com

Unit A, Whitacre Mews, 26-34 Stannary Street, London SE11 4AB

British Library Cataloguing in Publication Information Available

Library of Congress Cataloging-in-Publication Data

ISBN 978-1-4422-5140-3 (cloth : alk. paper) -- ISBN 978-1-4422-5142-7 (pbk. : alk. paper) -- ISBN 978-1-4422-5141-0 (electronic)

∞ ™ The paper used in this publication meets the minimum requirements of American National Standard for Information Sciences Permanence of Paper for Printed Library Materials, ANSI/NISO Z39.48-1992.

Printed in the United States of America

CONTENTS

1

BACKGROUND AND INTRODUCTION

The political position and sovereign status of the 50 states and the Alaska Native villages and Native American tribes differ in a number of important ways; however, the responsibilities of both state and tribal government toward their citizens present many of the same (and often overlapping) challenges and opportunities. As a result, collaborative policy development at the state and tribal level makes sense. In order for meaningful collaboration to become a reality, it is important for state policymakers to have a basic understanding of federal Indian law and policy, and for both state and tribal government to understand the benefits of cooperation. Gone are the days when policies affecting tribal populations were solely the domain of the federal government. Successful tribal self-governance initiatives, devolution of federal funding and program implementation to the state and tribal level, and an increasing awareness among state policymakers of the needs of tribal populations have all increased the need for more resources designed to promote successful intergovernmental collaboration. This book is intended to be one such resource.

State and tribal policymakers desire to move beyond historical mistrust and conflict toward respectful and meaningful partnerships. Moreover, state policymakers have a responsibility to meet the needs of tribal citizens within their states the same as they are responsible for meeting the needs of any other citizen. Working collaboratively with tribal government will increase the chances that the needs of tribal populations will be effectively served. There are legal implications surrounding tribes and tribal members, however, which differ from any other population of citizens in the United States. State policymakers must understand this legal status and how it came to be when developing programs and policy affecting tribal populations. As state policymakers become more familiar with tribal government and the benefits associated with cooperative policy development, conflicts can be averted, resources can be used more wisely, and policies can be made more effective.

Specifically, this book strives to provide policymakers at all levels of state and local government with a better understanding of the potential impact of state policy on tribal populations and help them steer clear of conflict—and potentially litigation—that can result from policies that are developed without communication or consultation with tribal government. To further this goal, this book contains information on tribal sovereignty and the legal status of tribes, an overview of federal Indian policies in the United States, basic strategies for state-tribal consultation, information on intergovernmental agreements and limited waivers of sovereign immunity, and an overview of federal Indian law areas that can arise as state policy is developed.

TRIBAL POPULATIONS IN THE UNITED STATES

According to the 2010 Census, 5.2 million people in the United States identified themselves as American Indian or Alaska Native, either alone or in combination with another race. Among this population, 2.9 million Americans identified themselves as American Indian or Alaska Native alone. This population is one of the fastest-growing minority groups in the United States, having increased by 39 percent since 2000.[1] Moreover, 566 federally recognized tribal entities are eligible for funding and services from the Bureau of Indian Affairs (BIA) by virtue of their status as Indian Tribes.[2] These tribes or Indian entities are located within the boundaries of 33 states. In addition, there are at least 64 state-recognized tribes in 14 states across the United States, and there are currently 68 Native Americans or Alaska Natives serving in the state legislatures in 19 states.[3] These numbers illustrate the need for state policymakers throughout the United States to engage in meaningful consultation and to work cooperatively with tribal citizens and government as a means of improving state law and policy.

Textbox 1.1 **Status of Land in Indian Country**

A federal Indian reservation is an area of land reserved for a tribe(s) under treaty or other agreement with the United States, executive order, federal statute, or administrative action establishing a permanent tribal homeland. The federal government holds title to the land in trust on behalf of the tribe. This land is commonly referred to as tribal trust land.

Fee land refers to privately owned, nontrust land within the exterior boundaries of a reservation.

Source: Department of the Interior, Bureau of Indian Affairs

TRIBAL SOVEREIGNTY AND THE POLITICAL STATUS OF TRIBES

The sovereign status of tribal governments predates the formation of the United States, and this status is recognized in the U.S. Constitution, federal statutes, and numerous court cases throughout U.S. history. The early settlers' practice of recognizing tribes as sovereign political entities has resulted in a unique situation by which Native Americans today are

> citizens of the United States, the states wherein they live, and . . . citizens of their individual tribes. Consequently, Indian people and Indian tribes have a political status vis-à-vis the United States that other U.S. citizens do not. Thus, when the U.S. enacts laws that benefit or harm Indians and/or tribal governments it does not raise issues of "affirmative action" or questions whether the United States is preferring one racial group over another. This is so because federal laws directed at Indians and tribes are based on the political status of the citizenship of Indians and the sovereign status of tribal governments.[4]

In other words, actions taken by the U.S. government in relation to the tribes are considered political in nature, as opposed to being race based.

The legal relationship between the tribes and the federal government was established through a series of Supreme Court cases—known as the Marshall Trilogy—decided early on in the history of the United States. These cases, authored by Chief Justice John Marshall, adopted the Doctrine of Discovery into the federal common law recognizing the European settlers' claims over the land occupied by the tribes;[5] categorized the tribes as domestic, dependent nations;[6] and recognized that state law can have no effect on tribal land without consent of the tribe or in accordance with federal law.[7]

These rulings, and the circumstances surrounding the relationship between the Native American tribes and the United States, gave rise to the creation of a "trust responsibility." This is a legal obligation under which the United States "has charged itself with moral obligations of the highest responsibility and trust"[8] in exchange for the millions of acres of land ceded by the Native American tribes to the federal government, which allowed for the creation of this country. This trust responsibility was first referred to in early Supreme Court rulings beginning with *Cherokee Nation v. Georgia*,[9] the second case in the Marshall Trilogy, and explicitly clarified many years later in the Supreme Court case of *Seminole Nation v. United States*.[10] The trust responsibility entails a legally enforceable fiduciary obligation on the part of the federal government to protect tribal treaty rights, lands, assets, and resources, as well as a duty to carry out the mandates of federal law with respect to American Indian and Alaska Native tribes and villages.[11] The conduct of the federal government and those acting on its behalf "should therefore be judged by the most exacting fiduciary standards."[12] Whether or not this trust responsibility has been honored or appropriately enforced, however, is a matter of great contention and debate.

FEDERAL RECOGNITION

Recognition of a tribe's sovereignty, ability to self-govern and interact with the United States on a government-to-government basis, and to receive certain federal benefits is predicated upon the tribe being formally recognized by the federal government. Federal recognition is the formal acknowledgment of an Indian tribe, the sovereignty of the tribe's governing structure, and its inherent right to self-determination. Federal recognition necessitates a government-to-government relationship between the Unites States and the tribe, and the federal trust responsibility requires that the sovereignty of tribal government be protected.[13] As a result, a federally recognized tribe has sovereign immunity (i.e., immunity of a government and its employees from being sued and the power of that government to waive this immunity in certain circumstances) and may exercise jurisdiction and its powers of self-governance, except as specifically limited by federal law. Federal recognition makes a tribe eligible to apply for health and social services from the Indian Health Service (IHS), confers federal trust protection, and confers eligibility for benefits such as job training, education, and housing assistance through the BIA. As previously discussed, the benefits provided to Native Americans and tribes as a result of federal recognition does not violate prohibitions on racial discrimination under the U.S. Constitution because the eligibility criteria is based on political status stemming from the unique historical relationship between the tribes and the United States, and does not amount to a racial preference.[14]

Federal recognition is granted through a regulatory process, subject to specific requirements set forth in the Code of Federal Regulations, by the Office of Federal Acknowledgement within the Department of the Interior. This process is referred to as administrative recognition and historically has been an extremely difficult and lengthy process. Numerous tribes have petitions that have been pending for many years. To address this problem, in late June 2015 the Department of Interior released its final rule revising the federal recognition process to increase efficiency, transparency, and fairness. In doing so, the new requirements carry forward seven mandatory criteria (listed below) that tribes were required to meet prior to the implementation of the recent reforms, while incorporating several important revisions to improve upon the process.[15]

The mandatory criteria include:[16]

1. Petitioners have been identified as an American Indian entity on a substantially continuous basis since 1900,
2. A predominant portion of the petitioning group comprises a distinct community and has existed as a community from historical times until present,
3. Petitioners have maintained political influence or authority over its members as an autonomous entity from historical times until the present,
4. Petitioners must provide a copy or descriptive statement of the group's present governing documents, including membership criteria,

5. Petitioner's membership consists of individuals who descend from a historical Indian tribe or from historical Indian tribes that combined and functioned as a single autonomous political entity,
6. Membership of the petitioning group is composed primarily of those who are not members of any acknowledged North American Indian tribe, and
7. Neither the petitioners nor its members are the subject of congressional legislation that has expressly terminated or forbidden the federal relationship.

Key revisions to the federal requirements now provide:[17]

- Uniform start date of 1900 for determining identification, community, and political authority has an Indian entity (the previous rule imposed different documentary requirements by evaluating petitioners based on first sustained contact),
- Prior decisions finding evidence or methodology (presented by past petitioners) sufficient to satisfy the federal requirements will be deemed sufficient to satisfy the federal requirements for a present petitioner,
- The Office of Federal Acknowledgement (OFA) will issue proposed findings, thereby offering petitioners whose claims face denial the opportunity for a hearing to address their objections before an administrative law judge, who will then provide a recommended decision to the Assistant Secretary,
- All publicly available documents relating to a petition must be posted on the Department's website and broader notice is provided of pending petitions to local governments,
- The Assistant Secretary will issue a final determination, upon review of the proposed findings and the any recommendations made by an administrative law judge pertaining to the petition, and issue a final determination for the Department. Any challenges to a final determination may be pursued in the United States District Court.
- • In order to promote efficiency, any petitioner that was previously denied federal acknowledgement under this process may not re-petition.
- • The newly revised process will serve as the sole administrative channel for tribes to pursue federal recognition.

In addition to being granted recognition through the regulatory process, it is possible for a tribe to become federally recognized through congressional action, though recognition though this channel is extremely difficult to achieve from a political standpoint.[18] A tribe may also become federally recognized through a judicial determination that results from a lawsuit in which a federal judge must determine whether the plaintiff qualifies as an Indian tribe for federal purposes, though this channel is controversial in that it raises issues of separation of powers between the branches of the federal government.[19]

HISTORY OF FEDERAL INDIAN POLICY IN THE UNITED STATES

The United States claims exclusive authority to deal with the tribes, referred to as plenary power, through two primary sources: the Indian Commerce Clause and the Treaty Clause of the United States Constitution. Congress and the Supreme Court have relied on this authority to develop and interpret the official federal policies that govern interactions with Native American citizens and tribes—policies that have varied wildly since the inception of this country.

Dating back to the early origins of the United States, there was an established practice in place in European countries and later, the United States itself, dealing with the Native American tribes on a government-to-government basis.[20] One of the most important considerations of the newly established U.S. government was to find ways to keep peace with the Indians, and as the Constitution was drafted, careful consideration was given to the place of tribal governments in the organization of the new government.[21] The United States continued the practice of recognizing tribes as sovereign governments when interacting and entering into treaties with them. As the population of the United States grew and the government became more powerful, treaties between the tribes and the federal government became more one-sided and less favorable to the tribes.[22] What followed were several distinct federal policies governing interactions with the tribes that include (1) Removal Era, (2) Reservation Era, (3) Allotment and Assimilation Era, (4) Indian Reorganization Era, (5) Termination Era, and (6) Self-Determination Era. While a detailed examination of the history of federal Indian policy is beyond the scope of this book, a high-level overview of these policies is included below to provide historical context.

The Removal Era ranged from approximately 1825 to 1850. Congress passed the Removal Act in 1830. This Act, prompted by the desire of the growing non-Indian population of the United States for more land, forced tribes to move west of the Mississippi River into what is now the state of Oklahoma.[23] In doing so, it was believed that conflicts could be diffused if the Indian and non-Indian population lived at greater distances from one another. Conflicts over land continued to arise between the relocated tribes and the non-Indian settlers, however, who began moving west in greater and greater numbers. In response, the federal government convinced the tribes to cede the contested lands and move further west under new treaties.[24]

The Reservation Era dated from approximately 1850 to 1887. During this time tribes were forced to give up their existing land rights and were relocated to designated lands, or reservations, set aside for them.[25] This time the hope was that conflicts over land and resources would be better controlled if Native Americans resided on lands specifically set aside for them, separate and apart from non-Indian settlers.[26] Again, this was not the case. As the population of the United States continued to grow and more non-Indian settlers moved further west toward California, demand for land and resources continued. Once again the federal government asked tribes to enter into new treaties and accept smaller reservations.

A dramatic change in federal Indian policy occurred in 1887 with the passage of the General Allotment Act, which divided, or allotted, tribally owned reservation lands into individual parcels that were then given to individual tribal members.[27] The idea behind this policy, known as the Allotment and Assimilation Era, was to impose an American or European concept of land ownership on Native Americans and assimilate them into the non-Indian population. This policy had the effect of breaking up large land masses that had previously been communally owned by the tribe, and "surplus" land was then sold to non-Indians—land that would subsequently become subject to state jurisdiction. This practice resulted in a loss of about two-thirds of the remaining tribally held land, or 90 million acres, from 1871 to 1934.[28] By the end of the Allotment Era, most Native Americans were living in poverty and severely lacking access to education and health care.[29]

The first half of the 20th century brought more dramatic changes to federal Indian policy, as it was apparent that the policies of the past had been, at a minimum, unsuccessful. The Indian Reorganization Act was passed in 1934 and was intended to increase tribal sovereignty and self-governance, stop the future allotment of tribal land, and encourage tribes to establish organized governments and written constitutions. This federal policy was short-lived, however, and was soon followed by a drastic reversal ushered in by what is known as the Termination Era beginning in the 1940s. Instead of supporting the development of tribal governments, as was at least the theoretical goal during the Indian Reorganization Era, the goal of federal policy during the Termination Era was to terminate treaty rights and the federal trust relationship and assimilate Indians into the non-Indian population as quickly as possible. "Federal lawmakers and BIA personnel believed that some tribes . . . were already sufficiently acculturated and no longer needed the federal government to act as their trustee. These tribes faced immediate termination. Other tribes . . . were to be given more time to acculturate before they too would be legally terminated."[30] The federal government terminated the legal relationship with over 100 tribes and, as a result, another 1.3 million acres of tribal land was lost to non-Indian ownership. This practice resulted in numerous negative consequences for tribal populations across the United States. In addition, the Termination Era saw the relocation of a large number of individual Indians from rural and reservation areas into urban city centers. This had the effect of further eroding tribal communalism.[31]

Termination was the official federal policy until the early 1960s, when President Kennedy refused to take action that would result in the termination of additional tribes.[32] This shift in attitude from the executive gained momentum through the 1960s under President Johnson, as millions of dollars were invested into tribal programs and infrastructure,[33] with the aim of addressing widespread reservation poverty. Finally, in a Special Message to Congress in July 1970, President Nixon declared that the "time has come to break decisively with the past and to create the conditions for a new era in which the Indian future is determined by Indian acts and Indian decisions."[34] Nixon's speech definitively ended the Termination Era that had previously governed the U.S. Indian policy and ushered in the Self-Determination Era, which continues on today. The federal policy of self-determination and self-governance has been

> advanced by an overlay of federal policies such as the "New Frontier," "Great Society," "War on Poverty," and "New Federalism." It was rooted in recognition of government-to-government relationships between the federal government and individual Indian tribes. This era has evolved in response to the demands of the Indian people and with the official support of every president since 1960.[35]

The primary goal of self-determination is to promote tribal control over planning and implementation of Indian programs, thereby affirming and promoting tribal sovereignty, and clearing the way for the development of meaningful government-to-government relationships. The principal law of the Self-Determination Era is the Indian Self-Determination and Education Assistance Act of 1975 (ISDEAA), which allows tribes the primary role in the governance of their territories and citizens and allows tribes to contract with the federal government for the delivery of federal services and programs to the reservation.[36] While tribal programs continue to be federally funded, the programs can be planned, operated, and administered by the tribes directly,[37] analogous perhaps to the devolutionary policies the federal government has favored over the last several years in relation to the states.

IMPACT OF DEVOLUTION ON STATE-TRIBAL RELATIONS

Many factors have prompted a greater need for state-tribal interactions over the last several years, including the devolutionary approach of the ISDEAA and, more recently, devolution over design and implementation of many federally funded programs to the states. While the government-to-government relationship historically has referred to interactions between tribal governments and the federal government, the shift toward devolving authority to the tribal, state, and local level over the last 20 or more years has prompted a greater need for coordinated public policy between the states and tribes than ever before. Devolutionary approaches to policy and program development were advanced under President Reagan and gained in momentum in the years following his presidency.

> Devolution is based on the reasonable proposition that policy is best made at the smallest level of government capable of doing so. . . . As a result, states have more discretion, more flexibility, more authority,

> and more control over federal dollars—in short, more practical sovereignty—than they used to, and they are using it to rethink public policies and tailor them to local circumstances.[38]

Examples of devolution can be seen in a variety of policy areas ranging from transportation funding to the provision of human services such as Temporary Assistance to Needy Families and child welfare services.

> Of course, devolution has a history in Indian Country as well . . . [F]ederal policy toward tribes, formally at least, has been devolutionary. Self-determination—which is a devolutionary policy—ideally places power in tribal hands, reducing federal controls over tribal affairs, resources, and decisions. Indeed, one might see the self-determination policy toward Indian nations as a precursor of the more general devolutionary tendency in the United States.[39]

Devolution of the administration of many federal programs has increased the common challenges and opportunities faced by states and tribes and simultaneously increased the need for greater state-tribal cooperation.

States and tribes can maximize the flexibility afforded through devolutionary policies to establish or further develop strong working relationships needed to create successful policies and programs. Moreover, it is important for states to recognize that "capable and sovereign tribal governments advance state goals as well as tribal goals. No state has an incentive to allow the kind of poverty and economic under-development that has characterized Indian reservations for so long to continue to fester within its borders."[40] The political reality today calls for states and tribes to respect the governing authority of the other and take a collaborative approach to policy development that meets the needs of all individuals and families to which the state and tribe are responsible.

STATE RECOGNITION

State recognition is becoming an important tool in establishing and institutionalizing government-to-government relationships at the state and tribal levels. State recognition of tribes refers to tribes that are not federally recognized but have been acknowledged by state law, and that sometimes reside on state-recognized reservations.[41] In light of the fact that the federal recognition process is complex and time-consuming, and many Indian groups cannot meet the associated regulatory requirements, tribes may want to pursue recognition through the state in which they reside as a means of securing other important benefits. State recognition facilitates cooperation and communication between state and tribal government. It validates tribal histories and facilitates government-to-government interaction. State recognition can facilitate inclusion of tribal perspectives in the state policy process and provide a multicultural understanding among public officials and the larger citizenry. While the benefits provided to state-recognized tribes (compared to federally recognized tribes) are limited, formal acknowledgment of the tribe's historical presence in the state and of the tribe's sovereignty can help state and tribal policymakers move beyond historical mistrust and establish a new way of governing. State recognition is in line with this process and, as states have become more aware of the potential significance of state recognition, many have acted to codify it.[42]

There are currently at least 64 state-recognized tribes (that are not also federally recognized) in 14 states.[43] Within the United States' federalist system, states have the authority to determine how (or if) they will confer recognition upon a tribe within their borders, so long as state law recognizing tribes and conferring specific benefits in connection with recognition does not conflict with federal law.[44] "[T]he legal status of their reservations and the scope of their governmental authority, if any, is a matter of state, not federal, law."[45] The process for conferring state recognition varies from one state to another, but generally involves one of four different methods. The various approaches used by states to recognize tribes within their borders include:[46]

1. recognition through state law, which involves recognition of an Indian tribe through the passage of a new state statute,
2. administrative recognition, in which recognition is conferred by an executive agency,
3. legislative recognition, in which the legislature formally recognizes a tribe through a joint or concurrent resolution (without the passage of a state statute signed by the state governor), or
4. recognition through gubernatorial proclamation or executive order.

Recognition through state law legally commits the state to a government-to-government relationship with the recognized tribe(s), as does administrative recognition, provided the recognizing agency is empowered by state statute to confer such recognition.[47] Legislative recognition and recognition through gubernatorial order or proclamation, while politically significant, may not be sufficient to solidify the government-to-government relationship in an enduring manner. Legislative recognition does not carry the force of law,[48] and executive recognition can only be considered legally binding on the state if it is clear that the executive acted in accordance with power derived from state statute or the state constitution. In order for state-tribal cooperation to be successful, the government-to-government relationship must be institutionalized so that it is not subject to change from one set of leaders to the next. In short, the relationship must be one on which state and tribal policymakers alike can depend. States interested in developing stronger state-tribal relationships that have not codified their recognition process, or lack a process altogether, may wish to develop one.

TOOLS FOR STATE-TRIBAL COLLABORATION

States and tribes have frequently collaborated around policy issues of mutual concern, and there are benefits to increased collaboration in the future. State-tribal cooperation and related agreements can accomplish a variety of purposes, including "recognizing one another's judgments, deputizing the officers of each government to act on behalf of the other, creating joint plans, allocating revenues, contracting for the provision of services or technical assistance, and sharing information necessary for regulatory or law enforcement effectiveness."[49]

A number of tools are available—those frequently used are identified below—that can help policymakers structure and institutionalize their efforts. Although this book does not seek to provide an in-depth discussion of ways to structure and implement intergovernmental agreements, the forthcoming chapters include references to the various methods of cooperation and seek to identify policy areas that may benefit from their use.

1. State-tribal cooperative agreements allow policymakers to define the roles and parameters of the cross-jurisdictional collaboration. Cooperative agreements can be tailored to address a specific policy issue and individualized to meet local needs. Proactive consultation and cooperation can help ensure that policies are mutually beneficial for both states and tribes, can alleviate jurisdictional confusion and conflicts, and ensure effective service delivery to their citizens.
2. State-tribal deputization and cross-deputization agreements are law enforcement–specific agreements that can be implemented to grant tribal law enforcement officers authority to enforce state law within the boundaries of the reservation or enable law enforcement officers to act as their state or tribal counterpart when enforcing the law on tribal land. Such arrangements can provide deputized tribal officers with clear authority to arrest non-Indians on tribal land and help ensure effective administration of justice.
3. State-tribal cross-court consortiums exist in some areas and can promote greater understanding and communication among state and tribal court officers and officials. Established working relationships among judicial officials can alleviate jurisdictional confusion, allow for joint problem solving, and provide a more seamless approach to law enforcement and court administration.
4. Full faith and credit clauses in state and tribal statutes or codes may be implemented to ensure that court orders issued by neighboring jurisdictions are recognized and enforced outside the reservation and vice versa. Statutory revisions also may be needed to alleviate incompatibilities between state and tribal law, remove barriers to effective enforcement of the law, and remove structural impediments to increased intergovernmental collaboration.

2

STATE-TRIBAL CONSULTATION

Strategies and Case Studies

State-tribal communication and consultation at the onset of the policy development process is useful for a number of reasons. Policies that lack collaboration are likely to have unintended consequences, be less effective than they may have been had they been fully informed by state-tribal communication, or result in jurisdictional disputes. Policy disputes resolved through litigation are time-consuming, costly, and destroy relationships. Moreover, the courts are meant to interpret the law, not reconcile competing interests of the sort that can arise as policymakers figure out how to manage shared citizenry and neighboring jurisdictions. Regular communication and formal consultation, when appropriate, can help state and tribal officials resolve conflict and develop policies that promote shared goals for the future.

Consensus building and dispute resolution—necessary to the policy development process—are possible if the parties know how to talk to each other. Consultation provides a structure and forum for such communication. Several states have consultation policies that will need to be abided by should a proposed policy action trigger the consultation requirement. In many other areas, no such policies exist, though policymakers may nonetheless decide consultation is warranted. States do not have authority over the internal affairs of a tribe; however, action taken by a state government can have significant effects on a tribe, tribal communities, or tribal members. In such cases state-tribal consultation is warranted, even if it is not specifically required by state or federal law. An overview of federal Indian law areas that may be implicated in the development of state policy are discussed in the following chapters and are intended to help state policymakers identify and determine if an anticipated policy action is likely to affect tribal members or tribal communities, thereby warranting consultation.

Once a decision has been made to pursue consultation, it is important to give careful consideration to how the process is structured and carried out. For this process to be successful, it is important that the state does not impose unilateral expectations for communication and input on the consultation process. Collaboration on the consultation process is needed first so the parties may then collaborate on the issues. State policymakers may wish to consider utilizing established negotiation strategies or incorporating traditional Native American peacemaking practices into the consultation process to support their communications and efforts toward cooperation (provided peacemaking is a practice used by local tribes who are party to the consultation). A brief overview of these practices is included in the following sections. In addition, lessons learned from the consultation experience of states and tribes with an established history of intergovernmental cooperation, discussed in forthcoming sections of this chapter, can benefit the consultation process of states and tribes in other areas. It is important that state policymakers identify and work with appropriate tribal leaders and government officials to determine how to collaboratively develop a consultation format that respects community norms and the goals of the participants, and establish channels for ongoing communication that leads to increased cooperation in the future.

FEDERAL CONSULTATION POLICIES

There are a number of policies in place designed to facilitate consultation and cooperation with tribal government. At the federal level, the consultation framework has been established through Executive Order 13175, issued by President Clinton on November 6, 2000. This order directs all executive agencies and departments to respect tribal sovereignty and to consult with tribes as they develop policy on issues that impact tribal communities. Specifically, the order provides that consultation is required in the following circumstances:[1]

- regarding any regulation, legislative comments or proposed legislation, and other policy statements or actions that have substantial direct effects on one or more Indian tribes;
- regarding proposed action that may impact the relationship between the federal government and the Indian tribes; or
- regarding proposed action that may impact the distribution of power and responsibilities between the federal government and tribes.

Each agency is required to have a process in place that ensures meaningful and timely input by tribal officials in the development of policies affecting tribes.

These principles were recognized and reaffirmed by President George W. Bush via an executive memorandum on September 23, 2004, which required all executive agencies and departments to ensure that the agency's working relationship with federally recognized tribal governments respects the rights of self-determination and self-government.[2] More recently, President Obama reaffirmed his administration's commitment to Executive Order 13175 through an executive memorandum on November 5, 2009. The memorandum restates the requirement that executive agencies and departments engage in regular and meaningful consultation and collaboration with tribal officials in the development of federal policies that affect tribal citizens and communities, and that the agencies and departments have a responsibility to strengthen the government-to-government relationship between the tribes and the federal government.[3] The memorandum further directs the head of each executive department and agency to develop a detailed plan of action governing the implementation of the directives of Executive Order 13175.[4]

Moreover, on June 26, 2013, President Obama issued Executive Order 13647, which established the White House Council on Native American Affairs.[5] The purpose of the Council is to improve coordination of federal programs and the use of resources available to tribal communities. The Council is comprised of the heads of various executive agencies and departments and is led by the Secretary of the Interior. Through the White House Office of Public Engagement and Intergovernmental Affairs, the Council is to coordinate outreach to federally recognized tribes to engage in consultation and to develop policy recommendations that support tribal self-governance.

STATE CONSULTATION POLICIES

Similar in spirit and purpose to the federal consultation requirements, a number of states have formal consultation policies directing state agencies and departments to develop consultation protocols that promote cooperation with tribal government and acknowledge the government-to-government relationship. The specific requirements of the state consultation policies vary from one area to another.

Some states have long-established working relationships with local tribes and mechanisms in place to facilitate cooperation. One such example is the Washington Centennial Accord. Following formal recognition of the government-to-government relationship by gubernatorial proclamation on January 3, 1989, the Centennial Accord was established in August of that same year.[6] The Accord is a commitment to implement and institutionalize a government-to-government relationship and improve government services to tribal communities. The Accord indicates that each state agency is responsible for implementation of the government-to-government relationship when dealing with issues of mutual concern. In turn, tribal government officials agree to communicate with the appropriate state agency in a manner that upholds the spirit of the Accord. State and tribal officials review and evaluate the status of the government-to-government relationship at an annual meeting of state and tribal leaders. The Tribal and State Leader's Summit of 1999 resulted in a determination that a stronger foundation for state-tribal relations and increased collaboration were needed. In what has been referred to as Washington's Millennium Agreement,[7] state and tribal officials committed to strengthening the government-to-government relationship and working to increase understanding of the tribes' legal and political status as sovereign governments. In addition, leaders agreed to continue to work toward establishing additional channels of communication and institutionalizing processes intended to promote cooperative policy solutions, including the development of a consultation protocol.

A number of other states have also established consultation requirements via executive order or through legislation, including Minnesota, California, Arizona, Oregon, and New Mexico, which recognize the government-to-government relationship and direct the state's agencies to develop protocols for state-tribal consultation and communication. Wisconsin takes a slightly different approach in that there is no requirement for the development of agency-specific consultation protocols. Instead, the Secretary of the Department of Administration is responsible for consulting with local tribes via an annual consultation session.

In Colorado there is no state law requiring consultation with local tribes; however, the Colorado Commission of Indian Affairs has developed a guide to formal state-tribal consultation to assist policymakers contemplating consultation with tribal officials. This guide offers a number of strategies that may be useful to state and tribal policymakers across the country as they collaborate around issues of mutual concern, including considerations to help determine when consultation is appropriate. In order to determine whether proposed action by the state government will have an impact on the tribes that warrants formal consultation, the Colorado guide sets forth a number of questions for consideration:[8]

- Is the action, policy, or decision directly targeted toward the tribes?
- Is the action, policy, or decision designated to include activities in Indian Country?
- Are federal pass-through dollars designated for tribes attached to the action, policy, or decision?
- Does the action, policy, or decision affect, or potentially affect, tribal community interests?
- Have any of the tribes expressed interest in and/or concerns with the proposed action?
- Does the action, policy, or decision affect the distribution of power and responsibilities between the state government and tribal government?
- Are there any special legal considerations, such as jurisdiction in Indian Country?
- Are state policymakers dealing with any federal laws that affect tribal communities or citizens? Such laws include the Native American Graves Protection and Repatriation Act; the Indian Child Welfare Act; the Title IV-E Federal Foster Care Program; Title VII Indian, Native Hawaiian, and Alaska Native Education; the Native American Housing Assistance and Self-Determination Act; and the Violence Against Women Reauthorization Act of 2013.
- Is the state administering any federal programs that provide for specific "pass-through" or "set-aside" funds for tribes?

Once it is determined that state-tribal consultation is needed, policymakers must turn their attention to preparing and implementing the consultation.

CONSULTATION PLANNING AND IMPLEMENTATION

When developing a consultation format, it may be helpful to contemplate the consultation process in three distinct phases: consultation planning, active consultation, and postconsultation discussion and determination of next steps.

At the onset, state policymakers need to connect with tribal policymakers to communicate their interest in consultation and have a preliminary discussion on the proposed policy or action under consideration, including possible impacts to tribal government and citizens. Policymakers will also need to discuss logistical issues such as the date, time, and location for the consultation, the format, and identification of necessary participants. Once a commitment to consultation has been secured, further discussions should instruct the development of the agenda and format, the type of notice provided to targeted participants, and information needed in advance to allow for appropriate preparation.

The consultation must allow for an open and honest exchange of information so that problems and disagreements can be accurately identified and addressed, enabling a truly collaborative approach to policy development. Policymakers will need to jointly decide how to structure this conversation, which may involve roundtable discussions or the use of a third party to facilitate policy negotiations in a mediation or peacemaking format. In their book *Negotiated Sovereignty: Working to Improve Tribal-State Relations* authors Jeffrey S. Ashley and Secody J. Hubbard examine several case studies focused on the dynamics of the intergovernmental relationship between states and tribes around the country. In doing so they identify a number of issues that commonly facilitated strong working relationships that policymakers should consider as they engage in consultation and policy negotiations. These guiding principles include:[9]

- **Face-to-face communication.** Intergovernmental relations will likely become strained if the state and the tribe talk about each other instead of to each other.

- **Focus on the issue at hand.** Disagreements regarding other policy issues have the potential to derail negotiations in other areas if the conversation gets overly broad.
- **Recognize sovereignty.** To ignore tribal sovereignty is to end any hope for cooperation. Similarly, the tribes need to recognize that the state is a sovereign entity that has its own interests and goals. Cooperation will only emerge when the goals of both sides are taken into account.
- **Avoid politics.** To do so completely is probably unrealistic, but the parties need to keep focus on the issue and their common goals if mutually beneficial policy is to be developed.
- **Look to other levels of government.** Tribes oftentimes deal most frequently, and often are in closest proximity, to county and city governments. Communication should involve all levels of government necessary to ensure successful policy development and implementation.

In addition, policy discussions or consultations should include technical people who can help keep focus on the issue and the details that must be addressed. "Those in the trenches are the most knowledgeable about how a program should be run, what the technical requirements would be for each side, and how each side could be best utilized."[10] Including both technical people and policymakers with decision-making authority can help ensure that policy discussions result in action.

Upon conclusion of the consultation, the parties should agree upon next steps and/or allocation of responsibilities surrounding implementation of any decisions reached. Depending on the complexity of the issue, additional consultation may be needed. It is important that the parties discuss how future communication around the issue will be handled and what channels will be used to support ongoing collaboration. In addition, the parties will need to determine the appropriate method of preserving or formalizing any agreements that result from the consultation. A formal state-tribal agreement or memorandum of understanding will likely be needed to ensure that the roles and responsibilities are clear. Policymakers should consider whether they wish to include a severability clause, or agreement that if any term or provision of the agreement is later found to be unenforceable or out of compliance with state or federal law, the remainder of the agreement will still be valid. Finally, the parties may find it useful to include a clause providing for periodic review of the agreement to accommodate modifications that may be needed as circumstances change or to address problems that are revealed during implementation of the agreement.

CONSULTATION STRATEGIES

A number of strategies may assist policymakers to structure their discussion so that they are better equipped to identify mutual interests, build consensus, and develop collaborative solutions. These include established negotiation strategies, incorporation of traditional peacemaking strategies into the consultation process, and lessons learned from the consultation experience of other states and tribes.

Principled Negotiation

One negotiation strategy policymakers may want to incorporate is the practice of "principled negotiation" developed by the Harvard Negotiation Project. Principled negotiation is designed to help parties decide issues on the merits as opposed to decisions based on positions—or what each side says it will and will not do. The goal is to look for mutual gains whenever possible and to rely on a fair, objective standard (such as legal precedent, scientific evidence, evidence-based policy research, etc.) to resolve conflicting interests.[11] This strategy can be well suited to state-tribal policy deliberations in which cooperative solutions are needed to promote mutual interests and to address areas of common concern. In order for this process to work, the parties need to clearly identify and communicate their interests early in the process so it is possible to determine where there is conflict and where there is common ground.

Textbox 2.1 **Key Components of Principled Negotiation**

People: Separate the people from the problem.
Interests: Focus on interests, not positions.
Options: Invent multiple options for mutual gain before deciding what to do.
Criteria: Base the result on objective standards.

Source: Roger Fisher, William Ury, and Bruce Patton, *Getting to Yes: Negotiating Agreement Without Giving In* (New York: Penguin Books, 2011).

In addition, for policy development to be truly collaborative there must be buy-in from the necessary parties—namely, those with decision-making authority. One way to accomplish this is to ensure that both state and tribal officials have meaningful input into and feel ownership over the consultation process and the eventual course of action via joint brainstorming sessions. "[J]oint brainstorming sessions have the great advantages of producing ideas that take into account the interests of all those involved, of creating a climate of joint problem-solving, and of educating each side about the concerns of the other."[12] The goal of joint brainstorming is to develop a number of mutually beneficial policy options that may be appropriate to address the issue at hand. This allows for creative approaches that can be tailored to specific needs. To facilitate the development of mutually beneficial policy options, the parties will need to (1) separate the act of inventing options from the act of judging them; (2) broaden the options on the table rather than look for a single answer; and (3) search for mutual gains associated with each proposed approach.[13]

In instances where the state-tribal relationship has been contentious, or where a working relationship has never been developed, policymakers will need to find ways to overcome mistrust, negative perceptions surrounding state-tribal collaboration, or possibly frustration and hostility. This should be anticipated in the planning stages of the consultation, and the format should be structured in a way that allows parties to establish trust and acknowledge negative emotions associated with failed attempts to cooperate. In doing so, it is important to remember that relationship building and meaningful consultation is an ongoing process. Attempts at communication and collaboration should not be abandoned because difficulties arise. It is important to make emotions explicit and acknowledge them as legitimate, allowing each side to let off steam.[14] This is sometimes necessary in order to move beyond historical mistrust and conflict. Ultimately, however, "you will satisfy your interests better if you talk about where you would like to go rather than about where you have come from."[15] The past is important and barriers to future collaboration must be dealt with, but progress is possible only if policymakers can find common ground around their shared goals for the future.

Peacemaking Strategies

Another tool policymakers may want to consider when engaging in state-tribal consultation is the use of traditional Native American peacemaking philosophies to guide their discussions. State-tribal consultation that incorporates peacemaking principles may provide a framework for helping the parties identify collaborative policy solutions that advance their shared interests and help strengthen the government-to-government relationship.

Lack of trust or confidence in the state-tribal relationship thwarts efforts to develop policy in a collaborative manner. Peacemaking strategies may help strengthen the relationship so that ongoing collaboration is facilitated moving forward. Peacemaking strategies have been incorporated into a number of non-Native settings including the resolution of court cases and neighborhood and community disputes. Traditional tribal peacemaking philosophies can be useful in the public policy arena as well. The application of these principles in consultation involving tribal and nontribal policymakers may be appropriate given the focus on relationship building, open and honest communication, identification of common interests, and collaboration.

Peacemaking philosophies vary from tribe to tribe, though most peacemaking efforts usually share common objectives such as a focus on problem solving as opposed to an articulation of rights and obligations.[16] Peacemaking provides a safe forum where people can talk to resolve conflict in a way that addresses the concerns of all interested parties.[17] Peacemaking has been described as a "horizontal system" in which "decisions and plans are made through consensus."[18]

This should be the goal of collaborative policy development between states and tribes as well. Common attributes of peacemaking that may guide state-tribal consultation protocols include transparency in the process and flexibility, so that participants set the pace and shape the outcome.[19] In a peacemaking session, participants take turns speaking without interruption. The ultimate goal is to reach a consensus resolution that addresses the problem and strengthens relationships.[20] This is a building block for future policy collaboration.

From the onset of the consultation process state and tribal policymakers should discuss how to structure the consultation in a manner that appropriately accommodates the issues under consideration and expectations of the participants. Whether or not the inclusion of traditional peacemaking philosophies is appropriate can be part of this discussion. Should it be determined that peacemaking strategies would benefit the state-tribal interaction, consultation planners must consider how the concept of peacemaking translates to non-Indian participants and what modifications may be needed to ensure the format is successful.

Consultation protocols can provide the infrastructure to support meaningful collaboration. Incorporation of peacemaking strategies, when appropriate, can improve upon existing protocols or help policymakers develop an effective process where protocols are lacking. Efforts made to ensure the consultation process is effective make the difference between a process that feels like merely another layer of government bureaucracy versus one that truly advances a positive intergovernmental relationship.

LESSONS LEARNED

Analysis of the consultation experiences of other states and tribes can be helpful to policymakers contemplating consultation. Recent studies prepared for the Center for Medicare and Medicaid Services (CMS) examined the state-tribal consultation process in Washington, Oregon, and Minnesota regarding programs operated by the Indian Health Service, tribes, and tribal organizations under the Indian Self-Determination and Education Assistance Act (Pub. L. 93-638) or urban Indian health organizations under Title V of the Indian Health Care Improvement Act. Pursuant to federal law, states are required to consult with tribes and obtain advice from the Indian Health Service, tribally operated, and urban programs regarding implementation of changes made to its Medicaid and Children's Health Insurance Program.[21] The information derived from these studies, however, provides valuable insights that can be used to increase the likelihood of successful consultation efforts in other areas.

The three states that were the focus of the CMS case studies are areas perceived to have a history of successful state-tribal cooperation. Participants were asked to describe the strengths and weaknesses of the consultation experiences and the lessons that may be shared with others engaging in state-tribal consultation.[22] A commonly cited benefit to the consultation process by participants in all three states was ongoing, informal communication between state and tribal officials in the context of an established working relationship. The existence of these informal communication channels promoted open communication and facilitated cooperation in the context of formal consultation because the parties were used to working together. Conversely, a common barrier to effective consultation and collaboration was overdemand for consultation. In terms of consultation preparation, participants emphasized the importance of joint planning, transparency in the process, and ensuring that information and agendas are provided in advance so participants can adequately prepare.

In addition to the factors referenced above, there are a number of lessons learned from Washington, Oregon, and Minnesota, as described in the CMS studies, which may help policymakers in other areas engage in effective consultation. These include:[23]

- Establish a formal consultation policy that holds specific agencies or actors responsible for designated activities. This policy should be developed with tribal stakeholders and should be available for public comment and review.
- Regularly monitor and evaluate the consultation process to ensure that it fosters efficiency and effective interactions, amending it as necessary.
- Limit formal consultation requests to relevant, significant matters, rather than requiring consultation for every issue.
- Acknowledge the sovereignty of tribal nations while working toward shared goals on a government-to-government basis.
- Ensure ongoing training in tribal history, state-tribal relations, and consultation protocol for state and tribal staff, particularly those involved in the consultation process.
- Tailor communication so that the appropriate method is used for the intended audience (i.e., more formality will be required when dealing with tribal leadership, as opposed to staff-to-staff communications).
- Include state and tribal leadership to participate in the consultation process. It is vitally important that officials with the ability to commit to action are included and that policymakers of equal authority from both governments support the process and are involved in the consultation.

States that are lacking a formal state-tribal consultation protocol may wish to develop one. "By formalizing the consultation policy, the state demonstrates a public commitment to engaging with tribal governments, and tribes have a more significant process to call on during consultation efforts, thus providing a platform for true government-to-government interaction."[24] Implementation of a state-tribal protocol helps institutionalize the working relationship, insulating it from turnover within both state and tribal government and individual personalities or changes in the political climate that may be less favorable toward collaboration.

For the consultation process to be truly effective there must be accountability and follow-through on agreed-upon outcomes. Tribal consultation participants emphasized the need for consultation that leads to results. In response, authors of the Minnesota study recommend a module, referred to by the acronym SMART,[25] which is intended to ensure that consultation ultimately translates into action.

Textbox 2.2 **SMART Consultation Module**

S: Specific. Clearly define goals, expectations, and timelines.
M: Measurable. Determine how progress toward outcomes will be measured.
A: Achievable. Outcomes should be feasible and attainable given available support, resources, and timeframes.
R: Relevant. Outcomes should align with identified goals.
T: Timeframe. Identify a target date for outcome completion and for achieving certain milestones toward outcome. Should include delegation of responsibility for completion of related tasks.

Source: "Best Practices in State-Tribal Consultation: Findings from Minnesota," Kauffman & Associates, Inc., Spokane, WA.

An additional consideration for policymakers contemplating consultation is the fact that not all collaboration involving states and tribes warrants a formal consultation. Collaborative efforts, in some instances, may be best served by ongoing informal communication among state and tribal policymakers or staff. Consultation overload was a frustration to participants in all states examined by the CMS studies. State and tribal policymakers alike have limited time and resources to participate in formal consultation and, as such, it should be limited to issues in which it is required by law or when it is a necessary component to meaningful intergovernmental cooperation. Strong working relationships, as well as knowledge of federal Indian law and state-tribal relations, are needed at all levels of state and local government so that informal communication with tribal officials can effectively address issues as they arise and allow policymakers to determine if formal consultation is needed.

Finally, any type of interaction—whether informal communication, formal consultation, or policy development and implementation—between state and tribal government will benefit from an established working relationship, which takes time to build. The potential benefits to the policy development process, however, make the effort worthwhile.

3

SOVEREIGN IMMUNITY AND ITS IMPACT ON STATE-TRIBAL RELATIONS

LEGAL ORIGINS

Sovereign immunity is a legal doctrine that prohibits a government from being sued without its permission. The underlying purpose is to protect government assets from being subject to a judgment resulting from individual or class action lawsuits. Sovereign immunity is an inherent attribute of any sovereign government whether it is federal, state, or tribal. In the case of state and tribal government, explicit action by Congress is required to limit or abolish it. A sovereign government has the power to waive its immunity generally or in a limited capacity, subjecting itself to lawsuits in specific circumstances. The application of tribal sovereign immunity has similarities and differences compared to the sovereign immunity of federal or state governments. Understanding these similarities and differences can facilitate state-tribal cooperation.

Why would a government want to waive its immunity to legal action? There are several possible reasons. In some instances, allowing an individual the ability to seek redress for an injury resulting from government action is the right thing to do. Tribal governments, who frequently engage in entrepreneurial endeavors, may determine that limited waivers of sovereign immunity are necessary to promote economic development on tribal lands. Where state-tribal collaboration is concerned, limited waivers of sovereign immunity may be incorporated into the provisions of a cooperative agreement so that liability and recourse for negligent action under the agreement are clear.

The federal government and state governments waive their immunity under certain circumstances. Many tribal governments have chosen to do so as well. The Federal Tort Claims Act (FTCA) was enacted in 1946 and provides a waiver of immunity to allow individuals to bring a cause of action against the federal government for injuries caused by an act or omission of its employees, subject to specific limitations. In turn, states have enacted their own sovereign immunity statutes, typically modeled after the FTCA, that provide limited waivers for injuries alleged against the state. Some tribes have sovereign immunity statutes incorporated into their tribal codes which also set forth the circumstances in which the tribal government can be sued, though most waivers of tribal sovereign immunity are issued on a case-by-case basis through contract terms or through the provisions of an intergovernmental agreement.

The U.S. Supreme Court has a long history of recognizing a broad application of tribal sovereign immunity. As a matter of federal law, an Indian tribe is subject to suit only where Congress has authorized the suit or the tribe has waived its immunity.[1] Moreover, tribes are entitled to immunity for governmental or commercial actions both on and off the reservations.[2] If a tribe elects to grant a waiver of sovereign immunity, the waiver must be explicit and "unequivocally expressed."[3]

Tribal sovereign immunity, as with the sovereign immunity of any government, is intended to protect government assets used to serve the needs of the entire community. Limited waivers of immunity serve the dual purpose of protecting these public assets against fraudulent or unreasonable claims, while simultaneously allowing for appropriate compensation when government action has caused harm. The discussion of tribal sovereign immunity contained in this chapter is focused on two key areas: limited waivers of immunity for purposes of economic development and limited waivers of immunity needed to facilitate the formation of state-tribal cooperative agreements.

LIMITED WAIVERS OF IMMUNITY AND ECONOMIC DEVELOPMENT

Waivers of tribal sovereign immunity as it relates to economic development (i.e., business loans, commercial contracts, liability for injuries sustained by business patrons, etc.) have become an important issue as large-scale business development on tribal land has increased dramatically over the last 20 years or more. A tribe's sovereign immunity extends not just to their governmental functions but also to tribal business entities, as the Supreme Court has not "drawn a distinction between governmental and commercial activities of the tribe."[4] This situation can cause confusion, as it is unique to tribal governments. Neither the federal government nor the state governments engage in for-profit entrepreneurial ventures as tribal governments do, so the application of federal or state sovereign immunity to business enterprises is not applicable, and private, nontribal businesses cannot invoke the defense of sovereign immunity when subject to a lawsuit. Misperceptions can result without an understanding of the rationale tied to the extension of tribal sovereign immunity to tribal business enterprises.

Economic development on tribal lands makes self-governance possible. It is essential that tribal governments develop avenues for generating revenue that allows government to function, as they are lacking a taxable land base through which revenue would otherwise be generated. "Unlike state governments, tribal governments are generally not in a position to levy property or income taxes because of the unique nature of land tenure in Indian Country, fragile economies, and jurisdictional constraints. Income from tribal businesses is the only non-federal revenue source for most tribes."[5] The federal government has a responsibility to protect the tribes' assets, resources, and right to self-governance, in furtherance of the federal self-governance policy and federal trust responsibility, and revenue generated by tribal businesses is a necessary component of self-governance. "If tribal assets could be dissipated by litigation, the efforts of the United States to provide the tribes with economic and political autonomy could be frustrated."[6] As such, "[b]ecause concern over tribal economies is an important justification for immunity, it is not surprising that courts have extended the tribes' immunity to tribal businesses."[7] However, "[c]onsumers and other businesses may be reluctant to deal with a party that cannot be held legally accountable for its actions."[8] By granting limited waivers of immunity tribal officials can promote economic growth and counter any misperceptions that Indian country is an inhospitable place to do business. Limited waivers set clear expectations and ensure that everyone is playing by the same rules. As a result, limited waivers of immunity can promote economic development on tribal lands by giving both potential business partners and patrons confidence that recourse is available in the event that something goes wrong. Waivers of sovereign immunity that are well reasoned and appropriately tailored in scope "[promote] business relationships with nontribal parties, but by imposing limitations on liability, it protects the tribal treasury from excessive damages."[9]

LIMITED WAIVERS OF IMMUNITY AND INTERGOVERNMENTAL AGREEMENTS

Many policy areas require coordination among state and tribal government. State-tribal compacts, intergovernmental agreements, and memorandums of understanding can provide a road map charting policymakers' path to cooperation in regard to a specific policy issue. These agreements set forth the roles and responsibilities of each government. Waivers of sovereign immunity addressing liability for tortious conduct by government employees acting pursuant to the agreement may need to be specifically addressed to help ensure the collaboration is successful.

When tribal governments cooperate with the federal government pursuant to the Indian Self-Determination and Education Assistance Act (ISDEAA), for example, liability for negligent acts or omissions of tribal employees is addressed under the FTCA via an amendment to the ISDEAA. The ISDEAA authorizes tribes to contract with the federal government for the delivery of services and programs on the reservations under what has come to be referred to as "self-governance contracts."[10] "Taken together, the ISDEAA and the FTCA provide coverage for claims resulting from negligent or wrongful acts or omissions arising from a tribal employee's performance of functions pursuant to a 'self-governance' contract."[11] There is no overarching law that addresses liability occurring within the context of a state-tribal collaborative effort. In the absence of a tribal sovereign immunity statute that would govern conduct under a state-tribal cooperative agreement, potential liability of tribal employees acting pursuant to the agreement needs to be addressed. "Tribes may waive their sovereign immunity by a provision in either the tribal code or in a contract. . . . Many tribes today agree to limited waivers of their immunity when entering into contracts with other parties, and then purchase liability insurance to cover any future liability."[12] Provisions for limited waivers combined with the purchase of liability insurance are frequently incorporated into the terms of state-tribal cooperative agreements. When incorporating such a provision into a cooperative agreement, the tribe's limited waiver of immunity must be clearly articulated, as "[s]tate and federal courts have ruled that a tribe's procurement of general liability insurance is not enough, without more, to constitute a clear and unequivocal waiver of immunity."[13]

Too often tribal sovereign immunity is used as a reason not to enter into agreements or transactions with tribal governments; this does not need to be the case.[14] If policymakers are willing to discuss ways to best address liability concerns surrounding government employees, intergovernmental agreements can be structured to provide for reasonable compensation, when warranted, while protecting the tribal treasury and respecting tribal sovereignty. The Washington and Kansas law enforcement agreements discussed below (both enacted into state statute) include examples of limited waivers of tribal sovereign immunity combined with requirements for the purchase of insurance to cover claims alleged against tribal law enforcement acting pursuant to the statutes.

Law enforcement agreements in Washington and Kansas both include explicit limited waivers of tribal sovereign immunity and requirements that liability insurance be purchased to insure tribal employees acting in accordance with the terms of these agreements. For example, Chapter 10.92 of the Revised Code of Washington provides that tribal police officers are authorized to act as general authority Washington peace officers with the same powers to enforce state law, including the power to make arrests, provided certain conditions are met. Among these, the statute requires the appropriate sovereign tribal nation to submit to the state Department of Enterprise Services proof of public liability insurance and property damage insurance for vehicles operated by the peace officers and police professional liability insurance. The Department of Enterprise Services is authorized to determine the adequacy of the insurance on an annual basis. The statute further provides that neither the sovereign tribal nation nor the insurance carrier will assert sovereign immunity to preclude an action for damages under state or federal law, the determination of fault in a civil action, or the payment of a settlement or judgment arising from tortious conduct of a peace officer acting pursuant to this statute.

Similarly, Kansas statute 22-2401a authorizes tribal law enforcement officers to exercise the same powers of state law enforcement officers anywhere within the exterior limits of the reservation of the tribe employing the tribal officer, subject to certain conditions. The statute requires the tribe to maintain liability insurance coverage for damages arising from the acts, errors, or omissions of such tribal law enforcement agency or officers while acting pursuant to this statute, and the tribe must waive its sovereign immunity up to the limits of the liability policy. In addition, the insurance provider is prohibited from invoking tribal sovereign immunity up to the limits of the policy. The statute requires that the insurance policy be in an amount not less than $500,000 for any one person and $2,000,000 for any one occurrence for personal injury and $1,000,000 for any one occurrence for property damage. The insurance provider must certify to the state attorney general that the tribe has coverage in effect that complies with the requirements of the statute and must notify the attorney general if coverage terminates or no longer complies with the statutory requirements. Any claims brought against the tribal law enforcement agency are processed as if the tribes were the state, pursuant to the Kansas Tort Claims Act.[15]

ADDITIONAL CONSIDERATIONS

When discussing waivers of tribal sovereign immunity as a provision of a state-tribal cooperative agreement, it is important that state policymakers understand the considerations that tribal officials must weigh as they determine the scope of any possible waiver. Tribes must balance the need for limited waivers so that responsibility for acts carried out in accordance with the agreement is clear, while also ensuring that immunity is sufficiently limited so as to protect (sometimes scarce) tribal assets. Intergovernmental agreements must be constructed in a way that respects tribal sovereignty and the right to self-governance, regardless of whether the agreement includes a waiver of sovereign immunity. Nontribal parties involved in the negotiation of these agreements "cannot underestimate the cultural and political significance of immunity waivers. That said . . . tribes [may be] willing to offer limited waivers for appropriately invaluable contract terms."[16] This can be a charged issue in Indian country, as waivers of sovereign immunity are sometimes misunderstood to be waivers of tribal sovereignty. In reality, limited waivers of sovereign immunity that further the long-term goals of a tribal government (whether to promote tribal economic development or improved state-tribal relations and good governance) are a sound exercise of the tribe's sovereignty.[17] All governments face circumstances in which waivers of sovereign immunity are in their best interest. Where intergovernmental agreements are concerned, tribal officials will need to determine how broad a waiver to grant to accomplish their goals. The scope of the waiver must be proactively defined, specifying under what circumstances immunity is waived, how liability claims pursuant to the cooperative agreement will be handled, and the maximum amount recoverable. Oftentimes the waivers of immunity coincide with the limits of liability insurance required under the agreement, as illustrated in the examples from Washington and Kansas contained in previous sections of this chapter. It is useful to keep in mind that the self-governance capabilities of a tribe must be strong before the parties can effectively enter into cooperative agreements that require a waiver of immunity, which is itself a sophisticated exercise of tribal sovereignty.[18] Much as each state-tribal agreement is uniquely constructed to address specific issues and concerns, waivers of sovereign immunity (as an important component of these agreements) must be appropriately tailored to facilitate the goals of the collaborative effort.

4

CRIMINAL JURISDICTION

Criminal jurisdiction in Indian country is a complex issue. It is necessary to understand the interplay of a number of federal statutes to determine which government—federal, tribal, or state—has authority and responsibility to respond to crime and other public safety issues. These include the General Crimes Act, the Major Crimes Act, Public Law 83-280, and more recently, the Tribal Law and Order Act and the 2013 reauthorization of the Violence Against Women Act. These federal laws recognize or confer jurisdiction to either the tribal, state, or federal government (or some combination of both) depending on the circumstances and individuals involved. An in-depth discussion of these statutes and the case law interpreting them is beyond the scope of this book. However, an overview of the jurisdictional framework established by these laws is provided to give policymakers a working understanding of criminal jurisdiction in Indian country so that areas for state-tribal cooperation may be more readily identified, facilitating the development of mutually beneficial public policy.

ASSERTION OF JURISDICTION

Jurisdiction over Tribal Members on Tribal Land. As a starting point, tribal governments have an inherent right to exercise criminal jurisdiction over their members, as an attribute of the tribe's sovereignty.[1] In addition, tribal governments may exercise criminal jurisdiction over Indians who are not members of the tribe when the crime was committed on that tribe's reservation.[2] A number of federal laws, however, must also be considered to fully answer the question of which government has jurisdiction over crimes involving Indians on tribal land.

The General Crimes Act, also known as the Indian Country Crimes Act, provides the federal government with jurisdiction over crimes in which either the perpetrator or the victim is an Indian.[3] This Act authorizes the federal government to extend all of its criminal laws into Indian country with three exceptions: (1) crimes committed by one Indian against another Indian (which are subject to tribal jurisdiction), (2) crimes for which an Indian perpetrator has already been punished according to the laws of the tribe, and (3) crimes that by treaty remain under the exclusive jurisdiction of the tribe.[4] In addition, the Major Crimes Act (MCA) provides the federal government with jurisdiction over Indians who commit one of the crimes specifically identified in the Act. Jurisdiction lies with the federal government regardless of whether the victim is an Indian or non-Indian. The enumerated offenses include murder, manslaughter, kidnapping, maiming, a felony pursuant to Chapter 109A (relating to sexual abuse), incest, assault with intent to commit murder, assault with a dangerous weapon, assault resulting in serious bodily injury, an assault against an individual who has not attained the age of 16 years, felony child abuse or neglect, arson, burglary, robbery, and a felony pursuant to 18 U.S.C. §661 (relating to theft).[5] The grant of federal jurisdiction under the MCA is an exception to the premise that crimes involving only Indians are subject to the exclusive jurisdiction of the tribe and is based on the belief that Indians committing major crimes should be subject to the jurisdiction of the United States.[6] Tribes are presumed to have authority to exercise concurrent jurisdiction over tribal members accused of committing one of the crimes specified in the MCA (the Supreme Court has not specifically ruled on this issue);[7] however, jail time and fines that may be ordered as punishment are limited by federal law.[8]

Although the application of these federal statutes is triggered by an Indian being involved, there is no statutory definition of "Indian" contained within the General Crimes Act and the MCA. The federal courts, however, have generally interpreted this to require that the individual in question have some amount of Indian blood and be a member of or have an affiliation with a federally recognized tribe.[9]

Jurisdiction over Non-Indians on Tribal Land. Crimes committed in Indian country by non-Indians against Indians are subject to federal jurisdiction pursuant to the General Crimes Act, as discussed in the preceding paragraphs of this chapter. Crimes committed in Indian country by a non-Indian against another non-Indian are subject to state jurisdiction.[10] The Supreme Court has ruled that, despite such crimes occurring on tribal land, tribal governments are prohibited from exercising jurisdiction over crimes between non-Indians.[11]

Victimless Crimes Committed on Tribal Land. Jurisdiction over victimless crimes occurring on tribal land (i.e., crimes in which there is no specific victim but involve activities among consenting adults that are thought to be harmful to society in general) depends on whether the crime is committed by an Indian or non-Indian. Victimless crimes committed by Indians will be subject to the jurisdiction of the tribe, due to the fact that tribes have an inherent right to exercise jurisdiction over their members. The state is prohibited from exercising jurisdiction over tribal members without specific congressional authorization to do so, such as that granted under P.L. 280.[12] Victimless crimes committed by non-Indians on tribal land will be subject to state jurisdiction.[13]

Jurisdiction over Tribal Members Outside Tribal Land. The state is entitled to exercise criminal jurisdiction over Indians who commit crimes off the reservation in the same manner as non-Indians who commit those crimes. A state may not, however, prosecute an Indian for engaging in a federally protected off-reservation activity, such as hunting or fishing rights.[14]

PUBLIC LAW 280

Application and Effect of Public Law 83-280. Public Law 280 confers federal jurisdictional responsibilities to specific states. This law provides specific states with criminal jurisdiction and civil adjudicatory authority—the power to rule upon civil causes of action arising on tribal lands by or against tribal members—in Indian country. The law does not provide states with civil regulatory jurisdiction. Regulatory jurisdiction is retained by the tribes.

P.L. 280 originally granted jurisdiction to six states that include Alaska, California, Minnesota, Nebraska, Oregon, and Wisconsin. These states are referred to as the "mandatory states" because neither the states nor tribes located within them had a choice as to whether they would be subject to the law. An additional 10 states subsequently chose to assume at least some degree of jurisdiction under the law. These include Florida, Arizona, Idaho, Iowa, Montana, Nevada, North Dakota, South Dakota, Utah, and Washington. In order for policymakers to fully understand the allocation of jurisdictional authority it is necessary to know if the state is a mandatory or optional state, if there are limitations or exceptions attached to the state's jurisdiction under P.L. 280, or if state jurisdiction has been authorized by any other federal law.

P.L. 280 states are authorized to exercise criminal jurisdiction in Indian country subjecting Indians to state criminal laws and prosecution in state court for crimes committed on tribal land in the same manner as non-Indians, except on those reservations that were specifically exempted under the law.[15] In addition to any state- or reservation-specific exemptions that may exist, P.L. 280 states are prohibited from taxing trust property or regulating its use in a manner that conflicts with federal law, and may not deprive an Indian or tribe of any federally guaranteed hunting, fishing, or trapping rights nor the right to license or regulate those rights.[16] Although tribes in P.L. 280 are generally recognized as having inherent authority to prosecute tribal members who commit crimes on the reservation, "[m]any tribes in P.L. 280 states . . . no longer have a comprehensive criminal justice system and rely instead on state enforcement."[17]

Another limitation on the state's jurisdictional authority under P.L. 280 relates to prosecutions for violations of the state's regulatory laws. States are authorized to exercise criminal—or prohibitory—jurisdiction, not (civil) regulatory jurisdiction. A state statute is criminal/prohibitory in nature, and therefore within the state's jurisdiction to enforce under P.L. 280, if the conduct it punishes is conduct that is never permitted (e.g., child abuse or rape).[18] Conversely, if a state statute permits a certain activity, subject to regulation, it is considered civil/regulatory in nature and falls outside the state's jurisdictional authority, even if the state law imposes criminal penalties (e.g., gambling).[19] It is often difficult to determine if a law is prohibitory or regulatory in nature. In making this determination, the courts have considered "whether the law contains exceptions to its enforcement, the severity of the punishment, and the extent to which persons or property could be injured by the activity."[20]

INCREASED CRIMINAL JURISDICTION OF TRIBAL GOVERNMENTS

Federal legislation has been enacted in recent years that increases the ability of tribal governments to address crime on tribal land. This includes the Tribal Law and Order Act (TLOA), which was signed into law by President Obama in July 2010. Recognizing that the complex jurisdictional scheme that exists in Indian country has had a negative impact on the ability to provide public safety services to Indian communities and requires a high degree of coordination among tribal, federal, and state law enforcement,[21] the TLOA seeks reforms intended to "empower tribal government with the authority, resources, and information necessary to safely and effectively provide public safety in tribal communities.[22] To this end, TLOA provides the following:[23]

- Requires the Secretary of Interior to submit a long-term plan to address incarceration in Indian country;
- Requires the U.S. Attorney in each federal district containing an Indian reservation to appoint at least one assistant U.S. Attorney to serve as a tribal liaison, and encourages the appointment of a special assistant U.S. Attorney to prosecute minor crimes, in addition to major crimes, in Indian country;
- Encourages U.S. Attorneys to provide technical assistance to tribal, state, and local governments that enter into cooperative law enforcement agreements;
- Authorizes yearly expenditures until 2015 of $40 million to assist tribal government in carrying out their law enforcement responsibilities, and $35 million for jail construction;
- Requires the Bureau of Indian Affairs to train tribal law enforcement officers in how to collect, preserve, and present evidence in cases of domestic violence and sexual abuse, and in how to interview victims of sexual assault;
- Requires U.S. Attorneys to send a report to tribal officials whenever the U.S. Attorney declines to prosecute a violent crime explaining why the crime is not being prosecuted;
- Establishes procedures to enhance the sharing of law enforcement information with tribal governments;

- Places special emphasis on juvenile crime prevention programs, construction of youth shelters, and care of juvenile offenders; and
- Authorizes Indian tribes to increase the sentence they may impose from one year of imprisonment to three years, and from $5,000 in fines to $15,000, provided that the tribal court proceeding was presided over by a judge licensed to practice law and the tribe offered free legal counsel to anyone indigent and sentenced to more than one year in jail.

The second piece of federal legislation providing for significant reforms designed to better address crime occurring on tribal land is the 2013 reauthorization of the Violence Against Women Act (VAWA 2013). VAWA 2013, signed into law by President Obama in March 2013, recognizes tribal governments' right to exercise criminal jurisdiction over individuals—Indian and non-Indian alike—who commit acts of domestic violence or dating violence, or criminal violations of protection orders in Indian country.[24] This is an important and necessary exception to the rule established in the Supreme Court case of *Oliphant v. Suquamish Indian Tribe*,[25] which prohibits tribes from exercising criminal jurisdiction over non-Indians, given the high rates of domestic violence against Indian women. Statistics show that 34 percent of American Indian and Alaska Native women will be raped in their lifetime and 39 percent will experience domestic violence.[26] Moreover, most sexual assaults in Indian country are committed by non-Indians.[27] Given the severity of this problem, and the historical difficulty in appropriately dealing with non-Indians who commit crime on tribal land, tribal authority to respond to these crimes is essential. These new rules took effect March 7, 2015, but a number of tribes were selected for participation in a voluntary pilot project in which they were authorized to begin exercising expanded jurisdiction under VAWA 2013 sooner. Tribes participating in the pilot project include the Pascua Yaqui Tribe of Arizona, the Tulalip Tribes of Washington, the Umatilla Tribes of Oregon, the Assiniboine and Sioux Tribes of the Fort Peck Indian Reservation, and the Sisseton Wahpeton Oyate of the Lake Traverse Reservation. Much like the expanded jurisdiction provided under the TLOA, the exercise of expanded jurisdiction under VAWA 2013 is predicated on tribes meeting certain requirements. These include:[28]

- Protect the rights of defendants under the Indian Civil Rights Act of 1968, which largely tracks the U.S. Constitution's Bill of Rights, including the right to due process.
- Protect the rights of defendants described in the Tribal Law and Order Act of 2010, by providing:
    - Effective assistance of counsel for defendants;
    - Free, appointed, licensed attorneys for indigent defendants;
    - Law-trained tribal judges who are also licensed to practice law;
    - Publicly available tribal criminal laws and rules; and
    - Recorded criminal proceedings.
- Include a fair cross-section of the community in jury pools and not systematically exclude non-Indians.
- Inform defendants ordered detained by a tribal court of their right to file federal habeas corpus petitions.

Given the recent enactment of this legislation, it is difficult to tell what the long-term impact will be, though it is hoped that positive change will result. Together, the TLOA and VAWA 2013 provide important changes to the criminal jurisdiction framework so that crime can be reduced and Indian communities made safer.

INTERGOVERNMENTAL COOPERATION

A number of innovative cooperative efforts between state and tribal government can be replicated in other areas to reduce high crimes rates and improve law enforcement in Indian country.

Law enforcement agreements and cross-deputization of law enforcement officers can help ensure that non-Indians who commit crimes on tribal land can be appropriately dealt with. Examples of such efforts exist in Washington and Kansas and are more fully discussed in the *Sovereign Immunity and Its Impact on State-Tribal Relations* chapter of this publication. In addition, tribes with sufficient financial resources may contract with a local law enforcement agency to provide additional law enforcement to the reservation.[29] This strategy is most commonly used by tribes in P.L. 280 states that have not created their own police departments, so cross-deputization is not an option.[30]

In Oklahoma, legislation enacted in 2015 amended the state's Children and Juvenile Code to require notice to the appropriate tribe(s) within three days if it is determined that a child taken into state custody may have American Indian lineage or ancestry.[31] Jurisdictional disputes can be avoided or mitigated by state-tribal communication (such as that required by the Oklahoma legislation) regarding children that are alleged to be delinquent or in need of supervision so the state and tribe can determine which government has jurisdiction over any subsequent criminal or civil proceedings (such as proceedings subject to the Indian Child Welfare Act) involving the child.

Jurisdictional barriers have also been addressed in some areas through the development of extradition agreements. For example, in Wisconsin (a P.L. 280 state) the legislature enacted a statute[32] authorizing the state attorney general to negotiate agreements with any tribe within the state that has reassumed criminal jurisdiction pursuant to 25 U.S.C. 1323 to provide for the extradition of witnesses and fugitives. The statute requires that any agreements negotiated pursuant to the statute provide that the court of the sending jurisdiction, before issuing the extradition order, notify the person named in the extradition warrant of the right to a hearing and right to legal counsel; hold a hearing to determine that the person named in the warrant is the person charged with the crime or is the witness demanded; determine that there is probable cause to believe that the person named in a criminal extradition warrant was present in the demanding jurisdiction at the time of the alleged crime or that the person committed an act in any place with intent to commit a crime in the demanding jurisdiction; and allow for a reasonable time within which the person may commence an action for habeas corpus if the person contests the legality of his/her arrest.

Finally, cross-court consortiums can help facilitate cooperation and promote greater understanding among state and tribal officials on a variety of law enforcement and judicial matters. The New Mexico Tribal-State Judicial Consortium is one such example. The Consortium is composed of tribal and state judges and focuses on relationship building and communication so that conflict can be averted and cross-jurisdictional issues, such as Indian Child Welfare Act, full faith and credit, and extradition, can be effectively addressed.[33]

5

CIVIL JURISDICTION

The exercise of jurisdiction—both civil and criminal—is among the most fundamental functions of any government. In order to be effective, a government must regulate its property and the conduct of its citizens, levy taxes and provide public services, define criteria for citizenship and regulate elections of public officials, provide law enforcement and emergency services, and prosecute criminal activity that occurs within its borders. These functions are common to both states and tribes. In order to effectively carry out these functions, coordination with neighboring governments is often necessary—or at least beneficial—and intergovernmental cooperation requires a basic understanding of the other government's jurisdictional powers. As states and tribes enter into cooperative agreements and engage in collaborative policy development aimed at addressing specific needs, the roles and responsibilities of each government must be addressed in accordance with each government's jurisdictional authority.

This chapter provides an overview of the tribes' civil jurisdiction and the differing rules that apply depending on whether jurisdiction is being exercised over a reservation Indian or a non-Indian within the reservation boundaries. This chapter will also discuss the power and limitations of the states' jurisdictional authority over Indians, both on the reservation and off. The rules surrounding tribal criminal jurisdiction are discussed in chapter 4.

From the outset, it is essential that state policymakers understand that the tribes' jurisdictional power is derived from their sovereign status and that the federal government has an obligation to protect the tribes' right to self-governance in fulfillment of the federal trust responsibility.[1] "Tribal powers of self-governance are recognized by the Constitution, legislation, treaties, judicial decisions, and administrative practices."[2] Moreover, the "limitation on state power in Indian country stems from the Indian Commerce Clause which vests exclusive legislative authority of Indian affairs in the federal government."[3] As a result, state law is largely preempted. These principles formed the basis of the foundational 1832 Supreme Court decision in *Worcester v. Georgia*,[4] in which the Court ruled that state law is inapplicable in Indian country absent an express grant of authority from Congress. Though the law has evolved, making way for some significant exceptions to the original absolute ban on state authority in Indian country, the premise of this case is an important starting point as states contemplate ways to best approach collaboration with the tribes.

Exceptions to the *Worcester* ruling were carved out with subsequent Supreme Court rulings that likely were influenced by historical events that changed the interactions between state and tribal government—namely, increases in the number of non-Indian settlers residing in Indian country as a result of westward migration, and the U.S. citizenship of Indians in 1924.[5] As Indians and non-Indians began residing in close proximity, disputes over land arose, along with questions as to which government had authority to act. With U.S. citizenship, state jurisdiction over Indians was implicated in a manner that had not been relevant in the past, as Indians became eligible for various state services, subjecting them to state law in certain situations.[6] Subsequent federal laws and Indian policy created additional scenarios that further increased state jurisdiction in Indian country. These include the General Allotment Act of 1887, which established individually owned (fee) land within Indian country that is subject to state jurisdiction, and Public Law 83-280 (P.L. 280), which conferred on certain states criminal jurisdiction and some civil jurisdiction over certain tribes.[7]

Today, a state's authority to exercise civil jurisdiction in Indian country is not absolutely barred, but the circumstances that allow for its application are very fact-specific. It will depend on whether the individual whose conduct the state seeks to regulate is Indian or non-Indian, and whether the assertion of state jurisdiction has a significant impact on the tribe, tribal members, or tribe's ability to be self-governing.

This chapter seeks to clarify the jurisdictional authority of states and tribes in order for intergovernmental collaboration and cooperative policy development to be successful.

ASSERTION OF JURISDICTION

Jurisdiction over Tribal Members on Tribal Land. Tribes have an inherent right to regulate the conduct of their citizens occurring on tribal land. In situations involving only tribal members, the tribe will have exclusive civil jurisdiction. The tribes' jurisdictional authority includes both the ability to regulate conduct—known as regulatory jurisdiction—and the ability to rule upon civil causes of action between tribal members—known as adjudicatory jurisdiction. A tribe's adjudicatory authority over civil causes of action involving non-Indians becomes more questionable. A tribe will generally have exclusive adjudicatory jurisdiction over civil cases brought against a tribal member by a non-Indian for actions occurring on tribal land.[8] And it has been argued that concurrent jurisdiction exists in civil cases brought by a tribal member against a non-Indian—both the state and tribe have authority to rule on the matter—though jurisdiction in this situation is less clear, and recent Supreme Court rulings have leaned in the direction of limiting a tribe's civil jurisdiction over nonmembers. Lack of jurisdictional clarity can result in conflict between the states and tribes. These situations can benefit from state-tribal cooperative agreements and cross-court consortiums that facilitate communication and joint problem solving. Full faith and credit clauses may also be added to state and tribal statutes/codes to ensure orders from neighboring jurisdictions are upheld.

States generally have no civil jurisdiction over tribal members on tribal land—regulatory or adjudicatory—unless they are acting in accordance with a congressional grant of jurisdiction, such as jurisdiction conferred via P.L. 280, which applies to certain states and tribes. (Further discussion of a state's civil jurisdiction under P.L. 280 is included below.) States have limited jurisdiction over tribal members on tribal land who are exercising rights as state citizens or residents, as state legislation defines eligibility for state programs and benefits.[9] State-tribal cooperative agreements can be beneficial here as well to ensure effective service delivery to all state citizens, tribal members included.

Jurisdiction over Non-Indians on Tribal Land. Tribes will generally lack civil jurisdiction over non-Indians for conduct occurring on the reservation unless the tribe can demonstrate that (1) the non-Indian has entered into a consensual relationship with the tribe or its members through commercial dealings, contracts, leases, or other arrangements or (2) that the non-Indian's conduct has a direct effect on the tribe's political integrity, economic security, or the health and welfare of the tribe. These scenarios, which make permissible the exercise of tribal jurisdiction over a non-Indian, were articulated by the Supreme Court in the case of *Montana v. United States*[10] and have become known as the "*Montana* exceptions." If determined that a *Montana* exception exists, however, the tribe has authority to regulate non-Indians through taxation, licensing, or other means.[11]

Textbox 5.1 **Application of Tribal Civil Jurisdiction over Non-Indians**

A tribe may regulate the conduct of nonmembers on non-Indian fee land within the reservations if

- The nonmember has entered into a consensual relationship with the tribe or its members
- The conduct threatens or has a direct effect on the political integrity, economic security, or the health or welfare of the tribe

Source: Montana v. United States, 450 U.S. 544 (1981)

Since the ruling in *Montana*, a series of subsequent Supreme Court cases have further clarified that tribes cannot exercise civil jurisdiction over non-Indians unless the criteria in *Montana* are present, regardless of whether the non-Indian conduct occurs on privately owned land within the reservation,[12] rights of way running through the reservation,[13] or on the reservation generally.[14] Whether or not a *Montana* exception exists will be dependent on the facts surrounding a particular situation and can be difficult to determine. Moreover, case law has demonstrated that the tribes must meet a very high standard in order to prove that the non-Indian conduct they seek to regulate affects a substantial tribal interest, as required by *Montana*, by showing that the interest at stake is "demonstrably serious"[15] and that court intervention is "necessary to avert catastrophic consequences" to the tribe.[16] In short, in order for a tribe to exercise civil jurisdiction over non-Indians within the borders of the reservation, a tribe must show either express congressional consent or the presence of a *Montana* exception.[17]

These decisions are controversial, as they complicate and limit the tribes' ability to regulate the conduct of individuals within their borders. The exercise of civil jurisdiction is so fundamental to any government that the result of these decisions has led some to assert that they amount to a "judicial termination" of the tribes.[18] Because federal law has created an unsatisfactory situation in regard to the tribes' ability to regulate non-Indian conduct on tribal land, states and tribes can choose to work together to mitigate jurisdictional barriers and uncertainty by establishing cooperative agreements that ensure non-Indian conduct can be regulated as needed, and to promote an effective administration of justice.

There are, however, areas in which tribes have been determined to have civil regulatory authority over non-Indian conduct occurring outside tribal land. An example of one such area is environmental protection. Tribes are entitled to assert their regulatory powers over non-Indians whenever a substantial tribal interest is at stake in regard to their clean air and water regulations.[19] While federal law requires the tribes to illustrate that their interest in regulating the non-Indian conduct is extremely serious before jurisdiction is permitted, it is important to keep in mind that environmental pollution transcends jurisdictional boundaries, making it easy to envision how the conduct of non-Indians could implicate a substantial tribal interest where tribal property and tribal members are concerned. Environmental regulation is a policy area ripe for state-tribal cooperative agreements, given the transient nature of pollution-related problems and the likelihood of coordinated efforts resulting in more effective outcomes than what could be achieved by either government acting alone. (Further discussion of tribal regulatory authority over environmental protection is included in a subsequent chapter of this publication.)

States may exercise civil jurisdiction over non-Indians on the reservation so long as the state action is not preempted by federal law and does not infringe on the tribe's right to be self-governing. In order to determine if the application of state law in Indian country is preempted by federal law, it is necessary to consider the extent to which the tribe and its members are affected by the state regulation, the extent to which the federal government is already regulating the activity or conduct, the nature of the state's interest in enforcing its laws on the reservation, and whether the state is providing any benefits or services in exchange for the burdens the state is seeking to impose.[20]

Textbox 5.2 **Application of State Civil Jurisdiction in Indian Country**

State law may be applied in Indian country only when the exercise of state jurisdiction

- Has been authorized by Congress
- Does not infringe on the right of Indians to govern themselves
- Has not been preempted by federal law

Source: Williams v. Lee, 358 U.S. 217 (1959)

A state regulation infringes on a tribe's ability to self-govern, and is therefore prohibited, if the application of state law impedes the right of the tribe to make decisions regarding internal tribal affairs—or infringes on the right of Indians to be self-governing. This criterion has come to be known as the "infringement test" and was established in the Supreme Court case of *Williams v. Lee*.[21] The prohibition against the application of state law that infringes upon the tribes' ability to regulate internal affairs applies even in states subject to P.L. 280.[22]

Jurisdiction over Tribal Members Outside Tribal Land. Tribes will generally lack civil jurisdiction over tribal members for conduct or activity occurring off the reservation unless the activity is governed by a federal law conferring such jurisdiction. A key example includes the presumption in favor of tribal jurisdiction over children domiciled off the reservation involved in child custody cases governed by the Indian Child Welfare Act.

Conversely, states have authority to exercise jurisdiction over tribal members off the reservation, in the same manner as the state would exercise jurisdiction over any other state citizen, unless the conduct the state seeks to regulate is governed by a federal treaty or law, such as federally protected off-reservation hunting and fishing rights.[23]

Service of Process and Seizure of Property in Fulfillment of Court Judgments. Additional jurisdictional uncertainties can arise as law enforcement officers carry out essential functions necessary to the administration of justice such as service of process and seizure of property in fulfillment of court judgments. Each of these scenarios can result in conflict, given the potentially volatile reactions of individuals who are the target of these actions. Jurisdictional disputes can further add to the volatility.

Some courts have ruled that tribal members can be served with process on the reservation for conduct that has occurred off the reservation. However, other courts have held that service must be carried out by tribal law enforcement officers—not state officers.[24] Given the uncertainty surrounding this situation, state-tribal cooperative agreements and cross-deputization of law enforcement officers can help alleviate potential problems.

Jurisdictional authority is also unclear in regard to seizure of property necessary to fulfill a judgment obtained in the state courts. Generally speaking, a court may not seize property outside its jurisdictional boundaries.[25] Only a few courts have addressed whether state officers can seize property on the reservation for this purpose. Some state courts have ruled that the state has jurisdiction, while others have ruled that they do not.[26] Further, arguments have been put forth that seizure of property by a state official infringes on tribal sovereignty unless the state first obtains a tribal court order permitting seizure of property as a means of enforcing the state decree.[27] The lack of clarity regarding jurisdictional authority and the high potential for conflict in this type of situation prompts the need for state-tribal cooperative agreements or cross-deputization of law enforcement. It also may be useful to incorporate full faith and credit clauses in both the state and tribal statutes/codes to ensure that court orders will be respected by neighboring jurisdictions.

PUBLIC LAW 280

Application and Effect of Public Law 83-280. Public Law 83-280 (P.L. 280) confers state jurisdictional authority in a manner that differs significantly from that described in the preceding paragraphs, for states and tribes that are subject to the law. This law provides states with civil adjudicatory authority—the power to rule upon civil causes of action arising on tribal lands by or against tribal members—and criminal jurisdiction in Indian country. (State criminal jurisdiction under P.L. 280 is discussed in chapter 4.) There is a nearly unanimous view, however, that P.L. 280 left the inherent civil and criminal jurisdiction of tribal governments over their members intact, providing for concurrent state and tribal jurisdiction in P.L. 280 states.[28] State jurisdiction over tribal members outside the reservations is not affected by the law. In addition, the law does not provide states with civil regulatory jurisdiction. This authority is retained by the tribes and includes the power to levy taxes, zone tribal land, and regulate the internal affairs of the tribe. The distinction between civil regulatory jurisdiction and criminal jurisdiction (authority to prohibit certain types of activities or behavior as opposed to merely regulating or restricting them in some manner) is oftentimes difficult to discern, as some regulatory laws can carry criminal penalties. This distinction is important, however, as it will determine whether or not the state has authority to act. Finally, P.L. 280 does not affect the trust status of tribal land, affect tribal members' eligibility for federal Indian programs, or waive a tribe's sovereign immunity from lawsuit.[29]

Although P.L. 280 grants states civil adjudicatory authority, a state court is not permitted to adjudicate matters over which the federal government has exclusive authority. Matters involving treaty rights or trust property, for example, are preempted by federal law.[30] A state court also is prohibited from issuing orders that would infringe upon a tribe's right to be self-governing, in accordance with *Williams v. Lee*.[31]

Background and History of the Law. P.L. 280 originally granted jurisdiction to six states that include Alaska, California, Minnesota, Nebraska, Oregon, and Wisconsin. These states are referred to as the "mandatory states" because neither the states nor tribes located within them had a choice as to whether they would be subject to the law. An additional 10 states subsequently chose to assume jurisdiction under the law. Among these, Florida assumed the full scope of jurisdiction granted to the mandatory states while Arizona, Idaho, Iowa, Montana, Nevada, North Dakota, South Dakota, Utah, and Washington accepted more limited jurisdiction.[32]

The grant of jurisdiction to these states under P.L. 280 is a significant departure from the past. Prior to the law's enactment, the federal government and tribes shared jurisdiction, exclusive of the states, over almost all civil and criminal matters involving reservation Indians.[33] P.L. 280 was enacted in 1953 during the Termination Era of federal Indian policy, which sought to end the trust relationship between the federal government and tribes, thereby fully subjecting tribes to state law. The complications the law has placed on the tribes' ability to be self-governing is incompatible with today's federal Indian policy of Self-Determination, and the law has historically not been favored by the majority of the tribes.

When P.L. 280 was enacted, tribes could not prevent the grant of jurisdictional authority to a state under the law, despite the fact that many tribes were opposed to such an arrangement. Today, a state cannot assume jurisdiction under the law unless a majority of the tribe's members consent. This change is a result of the fact that P.L. 280 was amended in 1968[34] to incorporate a tribal consent requirement. In addition, the 1968 amendments authorized the United States to accept a retrocession, or return, of jurisdiction by a state. Whether or not the retrocession is accepted is within the discretion of the Secretary of the Interior.[35] Since the 1968 amendments, no tribe has consented to a grant of state jurisdiction under P.L. 280[36] and retrocession has returned jurisdiction to approximately 30 tribes.[37] Indeed, some states have enacted legislation to govern the retrocession process. In Washington legislation was enacted in 2012,[38] directing the governing body of a tribe wishing to initiate civil and/or criminal retrocession to submit a resolution to the state governor, accompanied by information on the tribe's plan regarding the exercise of jurisdiction following the proposed retrocession. Requesting tribes are encouraged to collaborate with local government to ensure the best interests of the tribe and surrounding communities are served by the retrocession process.

In the years since the enactment of P.L. 280, both the tribes and the states have had numerous complaints about the practical effect of the law.

> Tribal concerns center around a belief that the law infringes on tribal sovereignty, that state law enforcement fail to respond or fail to respond in a timely manner to incidents on tribal land requiring the assistance of law enforcement, that federal officials have failed to support concurrent tribal jurisdictional and law enforcement authority, and that a lack of effective law enforcement on tribal land has resulted from the enactment of P.L. 280. In addition, concerns exist surrounding the perception that state law enforcement officers behave in a discriminatory and culturally insensitive manner when they do respond to incidents on tribal land, and that confusion exists as to which government is responsible for providing law enforcement services.[39]

States have also been critical of P.L. 280 in that the law conferred no state authority to levy taxes on tribal members or tribal land, thereby precluding a significant source of funding for law enforcement,[40] nor were federal funds provided to support the increased responsibility of state law enforcement. State officials have also cited problems in carrying out law enforcement responsibilities due to uncertainty about the scope of the state's jurisdictional authority and unfamiliarity with tribal communities they are responsible for serving.[41]

State-tribal cooperative agreements can be useful in addressing the problems experienced as a result of P.L. 280. Cooperative agreements can clarify the role and responsibilities of law enforcement. Deputization or cross-deputization can alleviate some of the confusion as to which agency—state or tribal—has the authority to act and ensure that non-Indian conduct can be immediately addressed. And cross-court consortiums can facilitate communication and effective working relationships among state and tribal courts to ensure the law is upheld. Collaborative efforts between state and tribal government have proven to be beneficial in a number of ways. Benefits include faster law enforcement response times, more effective coordination between state and tribal police departments, more jurisdictional certainty, and greater cultural understanding among state officials who may otherwise be unfamiliar with tribal communities.[42]

The exercise of civil jurisdiction—particularly regulatory jurisdiction—is broad, and jurisdictional uncertainty is common, both in states subject to P.L. 280 and in those that are not. There are a number of policy areas in which state-tribal collaboration and cooperative agreements can clarify and facilitate the exercise of each government's civil jurisdictional authority, including taxation, Indian gaming, environmental regulation, and child welfare. An overview of the jurisdictional framework and state-tribal cooperation in the context of these policy areas and others is discussed in the following chapters of this publication.

6

TAXATION

The power to levy taxes is a fundamental function of any government and is necessary to generate revenue needed to support essential government services such as roads and infrastructure, law enforcement and emergency services, and education and human services. Conflicts arise as the taxing authority of state and tribal governments overlap, and jurisdictional uncertainty and enforcement complications have resulted in litigation in the past. As is the case with state-tribal conflicts in other areas, disputes surrounding taxation are often better resolved through communication and cooperation—as opposed to litigation—which is costly, time-consuming, and damaging to the government-to-government relationship. The power to levy taxes (and limitations placed on that authority) can be an emotionally charged issue, given the vital resources tax dollars support. Fortunately, agreements can be structured to address specific concerns and advance shared interests in maximizing revenue and promoting economic development. The taxation authority of state and tribal governments has been the subject of extensive litigation, but also the subject of many cooperative agreements. Existing agreements can be instructive to policymakers contemplating the development of agreements where none previously existed or to address new issues as they emerge. This chapter provides an overview of the taxation structure in Indian country so that issues warranting state-tribal collaboration can be more readily identified.

LEGAL AUTHORITY TO TAX

The law governing taxation of tribes and tribal members, much like the laws governing other issues in Indian country, are complex, and misunderstanding is not uncommon. Increased understanding can help policymakers be proactive in averting conflict and pursuing state-tribal collaboration that results in mutually beneficial public policy. "The rumors of tax-free Native America have been greatly exaggerated. Individual tribal members generally pay [federal] taxes like any other American. With regard to state taxes, however, tribes and tribal members cannot be taxed by states or counties in Indian country as a function of [tribal] sovereignty."[1] Working from this premise, there are, however, important exemptions and nuances that apply to taxation of tribes and tribal members that state policymakers should be aware of so that common interests and concerns can be efficiently addressed. In addition, the law in this area is evolving, as tribal business ventures rapidly expand along with the growing number of non-Indians doing business on tribal land. "[T]axing authorities and tribes are constantly confronted with matters of first impression."[2] In light of the changing tax landscape, state-tribal cooperation will be increasingly important moving forward.

Under What Circumstances Are Tribes and Tribal Members Subject to Federal Taxation? Revenue generated by tribal governments, much like that of state governments, is not subject to taxation. This exemption applies to income-generating activities that take place both on and off tribal land.[3] Tax revenue is an essential source of funding needed to provide a variety of public services. And unlike states, tribal governments are typically not in a position to levy income taxes or property taxes due to the often tenuous state of tribal economics and unique circumstances surrounding land ownership in Indian country. Income from natural resources and tribal businesses are most often the only non-federal source of revenue available to tribal governments.[4]

Individual tribal members, however, are required to pay federal income taxes in the same manner as anyone else, unless a specific exemption has been granted by Congress.[5] These include tax exemptions relating to judgment proceeds (i.e., money paid to Indians as compensation for the loss of their property), income earned directly from an individual Indian's trust allotment, income generated through the exercise of federal fishing rights, and tax exemptions on the value of trust land inherited by an individual Indian.[6]

Under What Circumstances Are Tribes and Tribal Members Subject to State Taxation? As a general rule, state governments are without authority to levy taxes on tribal government or tribal members on tribal land without congressional authorization,[7] and such authorization must be "unmistakably clear."[8] Tribal governments, as sovereign entities, are not subject to state law, and a state is prohibited from regulating any activity in Indian country where the regulation is preempted by federal law or the regulation infringes on the right of the tribal government to be self-governing.[9] ("Preemption" and "infringement" tests are discussed further in the *Civil Jurisdiction* chapter of this publication.)

The Supreme Court rulings in a number of cases have consistently struck down attempts by state government to levy taxes against tribes or tribal members without congressional authorization.[10] As a result, reservation Indians do not pay state income taxes (for money earned on the reservations), state personal property taxes (on property located on the reservation and owned by a tribal member), or state sales taxes (on purchases made on tribal land).[11] The prohibition on the state's ability to levy taxes in Indian country applies even in states subject to Public Law 280, as the Supreme Court has ruled that no taxing authority was granted to the states under this law.[12]

Congressional authorization permitting state taxation of tribes and tribal members has been granted in some circumstances, however, such as the authorization to assess property taxes on privately owned land within the reservations.[13]

Under What Circumstances Are Non-Indians Subject to Taxation on Tribal Land? Jurisdictional determinations regarding the authority to tax non-Indians on tribal land are often fact specific and involve a balancing of state and tribal interests. As a result, uncertainty is not uncommon. That being said, however, federal case law has clarified some issues surrounding the taxing authority of each government.

While state governments are generally prohibited from levying taxes against tribal governments and tribal members, they are entitled to levy sales taxes on non-Indian retail purchases on tribal land and purchases made by Indians who are not members of the tribe in question, provided the tax burden does not fall directly on the tribal government. As long as the state tax does not interfere with the tribe's right to be self-governing, both states and tribes are entitled to impose taxes on purchases by such individuals—even though this situation may produce a double tax burden on the consumer.[14]

Tribes may only tax non-Indians on privately owned land within the reservation boundaries if the tribe can prove the existence of a *Montana* exception[15] (i.e., the non-Indian has entered into a consensual relationship with the tribe or tribal member or the conduct threatens or has a direct effect on the political integrity, economic security, or health or welfare of the tribe).

Under What Circumstances Are Tribal Members Subject to Taxation Outside Tribal Land? Tribal members are generally subject to state taxes in the same manner as any other citizen for taxable activity occurring outside Indian country unless an exemption is provided by federal law.

COLLECTION OF TAXES AND PROBLEMS RELATING TO ENFORCEMENT

Litigation can clarify the taxing authority of state and tribal government, but it cannot fully resolve problems that arise surrounding the exercise of that authority—namely problems associated with collection of taxes owed to the state and the problem of dual taxation. This is best done through intergovernmental cooperation.

Two key areas that have been the focus of litigation concerning the overlapping state and tribal taxing authority are severance taxes levied against natural resources extracted from tribal land and collection of state taxes on cigarette purchases made by non-Indians on the reservations.

Income generated from the natural resources found on tribal land is a significant source of income for tribes. The Supreme Court has ruled that both state and tribal government are entitled to levy taxes on non-Indian economic activity involving natural resource extraction.[16] This results in dual taxation. The Supreme Court has recognized the fact that dual taxation will likely result in higher costs being passed on to non-Indian lessees doing business on tribal land, noting that "[t]he burdensome consequence is entirely attributable to the fact that the leases are located in an area where two governmental entities share jurisdiction."[17] For this reason, intergovernmental cooperation is useful in addressing problems that litigation has not solved. Agreements between the state and tribe addressing problems of dual taxation (possibly providing for a tax-sharing arrangement or state tax waiver) can alleviate the disincentive non-Indians may otherwise have for pursuing economic ventures on tribal land.

Similarly, the Supreme Court has ruled that both the state and the tribe are entitled to assess taxes on cigarette purchases made on the reservation by individuals who are not members of the tribe. (Sales to non-Indians purchasing cigarettes on the reservation from tribal "smoke shops" are common.) In addition, the state may impose "minimal burdens on Indian businesses to aid in collecting and enforcing that tax."[18] This puts tribes in a difficult position whereby they are legally obligated to collect the state tax, despite the administrative difficulties associated with it. And since tribes also are entitled to assess taxes on these purchases, dual taxation raises the price of the product and dissuades nonmembers from doing business on the reservation. Tribes may opt to keep prices competitive by forgoing the tribal tax in order to avoid dual taxation, but then the "state tax revenue flows exclusively off-reservation."[19] Because of this dilemma, tribes have historically been resistant to collect state taxes, and their refusal to do so has produced conflict and litigation. On more than one occasion the Supreme Court has ruled that the state is entitled to seize cigarette shipments traveling to the reservation as one possible remedy,[20] but this is a solution that generally will result in more conflict. And since tribal sovereign immunity prohibits the state from filing a lawsuit against the tribe to enforce its right to collect on these taxes,[21] both sides have an incentive to cooperate.

STATE-TRIBAL TAX AGREEMENTS

Numerous tax agreements have been established between states and tribes across the United States. Like any state-tribal agreement, each is tailored to address local needs, but generally speaking, they aim to resolve problems associated with dual taxation and with collection of state taxes on sales to nonmembers. Some of these agreements address competition (ensuring that product prices on goods sold on tribal land are roughly equal to product prices on similar goods sold outside tribal land), and focus on ways of maximizing revenue.[22] Different approaches to state-tribal cooperative agreements include dividing or sharing tax revenue, levying only tribal taxes, tax collection at the wholesale level, state refunds to tribal members, or exemptions for certain entities or individuals.[23]

For example, in the wake of the 1991 litigation in *Oklahoma Tax Commission v. Citizen Band Potawatomi Indian Tribe*[24] in which the state-tribal conflict surrounding taxation of nonmembers boiled over, state-tribal tax compacts were established between the state of Oklahoma and the Seminole, Cherokee, Chickasaw, and Choctaw Nations. These compacts provided that the tribes would assess a reduced state tax on cigarettes sold to non-Indians on tribal land, enabling tobacco retailers on tribal land to remain competitive with nontribal retailers, while generating tax revenue for both the state and the tribes.[25] These sorts of agreements can be very useful in helping state and tribal policymakers move beyond conflict and litigation toward cooperation by acknowledging the needs and concerns of each government and finding ways to realize joint gains.

More recently, an agreement was established between the Three Affiliated Tribes of North Dakota and the state to share tax revenue from oil and gas production on the reservation, including from fee land.[26] In New Mexico state statute authorizes the establishment of state-tribal tax agreements in which the state grants a 75 percent credit against state and local gross receipts tax due from taxpayers who are subject to both taxes provided the tribe grants a 25 percent credit against its tax and meets other specified conditions. The result is that taxpayers pay the same tax as they would under state and local taxes alone, thereby eliminating dual taxation.[27] And in Washington, the legislature has authorized the state governor to enter into compacts that allow tribes to keep 100 percent of the state's cigarette taxes so long as the tribe assesses the full state tax (ensuring that cigarettes purchased on the reservation cost approximately the same as cigarettes purchased off the reservation) and provided the proceeds are used to support essential government services.[28]

Agreements such as these need to be negotiated between the state, generally led by the state governor, and each tribal government. In doing so, policymakers will need to consider whether it is necessary for the legislature to enact an enabling statute,[29] conferring proper authority for a specific public official or governing entity to enter into such negotiations. Finally, in an effort to promote greater understanding of the tax structure as applied to tribes and tribal members, the Washington Department of

Revenue has developed a guide[30] to assist individuals doing business on tribal land. Policymakers in other areas may want to collaborate with local tribes to create and make available similar resources to facilitate understanding of this complex issue and to promote economic activity and development in and around tribal land.

7

INDIAN GAMING

Indian gaming is authorized by federal statute under the Indian Gaming Regulatory Act (IGRA) of 1988. It was enacted by Congress, pursuant to the Indian Commerce Clause of the U.S. Constitution, and serves to balance the right of tribal government to regulate economic activity on tribal land with the states' concerns surrounding by-products of gaming that can have impacts outside of tribal communities such as possible increases in crime, gambling addiction, and increased traffic to the reservation-based casinos. States also have an interest in seeing that Indian gaming does not undermine state law and policy on gaming. Intergovernmental collaboration is required under IGRA for certain gaming activities and is necessary to ensure that state-tribal agreements, or compacts, address the interests of both governments.

In the years leading up to the passage of IGRA, many tribes around the country were engaging in gaming activities on tribal land—some as a form of entertainment in the course of community gatherings and celebrations, some intended to generate revenue. As sovereign governments, tribes have the right to conduct and regulate economic activities on tribal land. But as gaming activities increased in scale, conflicts began to arise between the state and tribal governments over whether such gaming activities were allowed by law and who had the authority to regulate them. This conflict culminated in a 1987 Supreme Court case regarding the legality of attempts by the state of California to apply state bingo statutes to bingo operations on tribal land. The Court ruled that the state laws (which were deemed regulatory in nature, as opposed to criminal) could not be enforced against the tribes, since states are without the authority to exercise (civil) regulatory jurisdiction in Indian country, absent an express grant of such authority by Congress.[1] (States are prohibited from exercising regulatory jurisdiction on tribal land, even in states subject to Public Law 280.) Indian gaming operations began rapidly growing in number in the wake of this decision. IGRA was enacted shortly thereafter, setting forth federal regulations governing what would become a burgeoning industry throughout Indian country.

INDIAN GAMING REGULATORY ACT

The Indian Gaming Regulatory Act acknowledges that a key goal of federal Indian policy is to promote tribal economic development, self-sufficiency, and strong tribal government.[2] In furtherance of that goal, IGRA provides a statutory basis for the operation and regulation of Indian gaming.[3] IGRA establishes the National Indian Gaming Commission within the Department of the Interior to provide regulation and oversight to ensure that gaming facilities comply with the requirements of IGRA, applicable federal regulations, and tribal ordinances or resolutions.[4] In addition, IGRA sets forth different "classes" of gaming activity that may take place on Indian land and allocates jurisdiction over the regulation of those classes. An overview of some of the key provisions of IGRA is provided below to give policymakers a basic understanding of the Act so that state-tribal collaboration can be conducted in a manner that maximizes mutual gains and proactively addresses areas of disagreement.

Class I Gaming

IGRA defines class I gaming as social games played for prizes of minimal value or traditional forms of Indian gaming played in connection with tribal ceremonies or celebrations.[5] This type of gaming is not subject to regulation under IGRA, and regulation is within the exclusive jurisdiction of the tribal government.[6]

Class II Gaming

IGRA defines class II gaming as games of chance, such as bingo, played for monetary or nonmonetary prizes and authorizes this activity so long as these games are not explicitly prohibited by state law.[7] This type of gaming is subject to regulation under IGRA and regulation by the tribal government.[8] In addition, IGRA requires that the governing body of the tribe enact an ordinance or resolution regarding the regulation of class II gaming activities, subject to approval by the chairman of the National Indian Gaming Commission (NIGC).[9]

Class III Gaming

IGRA defines class III gaming as any form of gaming that is not included in IGRA's definitions of class I and II gaming.[10] Class III gaming includes slot machines, roulette, blackjack, and other table games played against the house. Broadly speaking, this type of gaming is authorized under IGRA if it is governed by a tribal ordinance or resolution approved by the NIGC chairman, conducted in a state that permits this type of gaming, and is conducted pursuant to the terms of a tribal-state compact entered into by the applicable tribal and state governments.[11] In addition, IGRA requires that tribal ordinances or resolutions governing class II and III gaming provide that gaming revenue be used to fund tribal government operations or programs, provide for the general welfare of the tribe and its members, promote tribal economic development, fund local government operations, or fund charitable organizations.[12]

State-tribal cooperation is an essential component of the regulatory scheme governing class III gaming. IGRA requires that tribes interested in conducting class III gaming on tribal land make a request to the state to enter into negotiations aimed at developing a tribal-state compact.[13] The compact governs the regulation of class III gaming and may include provisions relating to the allocation of civil and criminal jurisdiction necessary to enforce gaming regulations, and standards for operation and licensing of the gaming activity and gaming facility.[14] IGRA does not confer any state authority to tax gaming revenue.[15]

IGRA requires states to negotiate tribal-state compacts in good faith and authorizes tribes to file lawsuits against a state for failure to do so. Since IGRA's enactment, however, the Supreme Court ruled in the case of *Seminole Tribe of Florida v. Florida*[16] that this provision is unconstitutional in that it violates the states' sovereign immunity, thereby precluding a lawsuit unless the state consents. IGRA was designed to balance the interests of states and tribes in relation to Indian gaming, and the ruling in *Seminole Tribe* unfortunately tilts the balance of power in favor of the states—essentially allowing them to decide whether or not they will participate in compact negotiations necessary to establish class III gaming operations. "The Secretary of the Interior, in an effort to assist tribes to overcome the disadvantage created by *Seminole Tribe*, issued regulations stating that the Secretary could approve Class III gaming if a state failed to negotiate in good faith."[17] While a federal appellate court has held that the Secretary lacks authority to approve Class III gaming without a tribal-state compact,[18] the Supreme Court has not ruled on this issue, so the "efficacy of this . . . option remains unclear."[19] Fortunately, numerous compacts have been signed since this 1995 ruling, indicating that states and tribes are nonetheless finding ways to reach agreements.[20]

Compact Approval Process

Once the state and tribal government finalize the terms of the tribal-state compact, it is subject to approval by the Secretary of the Interior. Any compacts that have not been approved or disapproved within 45 days after submission shall be considered to have been approved by the Secretary, provided the compact complies with IGRA's requirements.[21] Compacts will not be approved if they violate the provisions of IGRA, other provisions of federal law, or the trust obligation of the United States.[22]

Gaming on Lands Acquired after IGRA's Enactment

Indian gaming operations must be located on Indian land, which IGRA defines as all land within the limits of any Indian reservation and any land held in trust by the United States or in restricted status for the benefit of an Indian tribe or individual.[23] One of the interests IGRA seeks to balance is the tribes' interest in establishing gaming operations against the states' concerns over the expansion of Indian gaming and new land being converted into trust status specifically for gaming purposes. To address these potentially competing interests, IGRA prohibits gaming operations on lands taken into trust after October 17, 1988, the date IGRA was enacted, unless certain exceptions are met. These include:

- The land is located within or contiguous to the boundaries of the tribe's reservation on the date of enactment;[24]
- The tribe had no reservation on the date of enactment (as would be the case with a newly recognized tribe) and the land is part of the tribe's last recognized reservation;[25]
- The land was acquired in a land claim settlement;[26]
- The land is part of the initial reservation of a newly recognized tribe;[27]
- The land is restored to a tribe that is restored to federal recognition;[28]
- The Secretary determines, after consultation with the tribe and appropriate state and local officials, that gaming on newly acquired land is in the best interest of the tribe and its members and would not be detrimental to the surrounding community. The Secretary's determination is contingent on the state governor being in agreement.[29]

INDIAN GAMING TODAY

Indian gaming has expanded tremendously in scope since the enactment of IGRA in 1988. There are now approximately 240 tribes that conduct gaming activities and, in fiscal year 2012, the Indian gaming industry generated revenues totaling $27.9 billion and included 420 gaming establishments in 28 states.[30] The need for state-tribal cooperation on this issue is apparent throughout the country. The requirement for tribal-state compacts under IGRA is the key focus of this collaboration and the mechanism in which both governments can ensure that their concerns are addressed. Failure to enter into good faith negotiations may result in gaming being permitted on tribal land without a compact that represents the state's interests and can result in missed opportunities for mutually beneficial economic development within the state. As discussed in the preceding paragraphs of this chapter, the Secretary of the Interior has issued regulations allowing for approval of class III tribal gaming operations in the event that the state refuses to negotiate a compact. While the legality of this channel may yet be challenged, the regulations pose a significant concern to the states in that a gaming license issued by the Secretary would probably provide for less favorable circumstances to the state than what might otherwise be negotiated through the terms of a tribal-state compact.[31] And more broadly speaking, stronger intergovernmental relationships and mutually beneficial public policy are likely to result in a variety of areas—not just gaming—when states and tribes work together to resolve their differences.

Since 1998, 78 percent of the tribal-state compacts submitted to the Secretary of the Interior have been approved.[32] These compacts vary in their provisions, with some requiring the tribe to share significant portions of their revenue with the state while others have no revenue-sharing provisions.[33] The compacts also vary in terms of their requirements for consultation and coordination with local governments—some require formal agreements that address effects from proposed gaming facilities, and others make no mention of agreements with local government.[34] Finally, while IGRA does not authorize states to impose taxes or fees on tribes (apart from the assessment to defray regulatory costs), the Secretary has approved compacts containing revenue-sharing agreements with the states "so long as the states provide the tribe with a comparable benefit in return—a benefit to which the tribe would not otherwise be entitled,"[35] such as the exclusive right to conduct gaming operations within the state or within a region of the state.

ECONOMIC IMPACT OF INDIAN GAMING

Indian gaming, in many ways, has been an important tool to tribal self-government and self-determination. Revenue generated through Indian gaming operations has translated into a number of positive outcomes, including seed money for economic development ventures which have allowed many tribes to diversify their business enterprises, funding to provide essential services to tribal members, and funding necessary to support tribal governance infrastructure. Indian gaming has proved beneficial to the economies of the surrounding, non-Indian community as well, generally through increased employment opportunities. While the economic gains are not equally beneficial to tribes across the board (tribes located near populated areas derive greater economic benefits), the economic improvement and diversification made possible by the success of many gaming enterprises cannot be ignored.

Since IGRA's enactment in 1988, unemployment on many reservations has dramatically improved. The unemployment rate for reservation Indians fell by approximately 4 percent in the 1990s and stayed relatively constant through the 2000s, while unemployment in the United States as a whole increased during the 2000s.[36] Other improvements, due at least in part to Indian gaming, include significant increases in per capita and median household income,[37] and the number of crowded homes and homes lacking complete plumbing has dropped since 1990.[38] And in terms of large-scale gains at a national level, the president of the National Indian Gaming Association indicates that "Indian gaming now adds more to the U.S. Treasury than the federal government spends on the Indian Health Service and the Bureau of Indian Affairs."[39]

On a more fundamental level, Indian gaming has, in many cases, allowed for significant transformation of tribal governance, very much in keeping with the goals of today's federal Indian policy of self-determination.

> Greater Indian control and economic self-sufficiency on reservations has been accompanied by rising social investment. Some tribes have improved or replaced their formal institutions of government through constitutional reform . . . [others] have constructed, reconstructed, or bolstered corporate boards . . . appellate courts . . . gaming commissions . . . and tribal administrations. . . . Until recent decades, these superstructures of tribal government reflected outsiders' view of how best to organize and use authority. But these reforms have brought alignment with local cultures, conditions, and preferences, thereby increasing the effectiveness of self-government.[40]

A number of economic and social disparities between tribal communities and the United States as a whole require policymakers' attention. Nonetheless, improved economic conditions, due in no small part to Indian gaming, have improved the quality of life on many reservations and also provided revenue that has allowed tribal self-governance to flourish. Strong tribal communities contribute to the overall health of the states in which they are located. Policymakers have a strong incentive to cooperate on programs and policy that will continue this momentum and address the problems that remain.

8

ENVIRONMENTAL REGULATION AND NATURAL RESOURCES

States and tribes have a common interest in working together to protect our environment and natural resources given the limited supply of many of these commodities and the transient nature of pollution. Congress has authorized tribes to assume primary regulatory authority for administering most federal environmental programs in Indian country, but the exercise of this authority can be complicated by several factors. These include confusion stemming from the differing scope of jurisdiction under the various federal environmental statutes; the status of land in Indian country which often consists of "checkerboarded" tribal trust land and privately owned, fee land; and the presence of non-Indians on tribal land whose actions may have an adverse environmental impact. In addition, states have historically been concerned about the off-reservation impact of tribal environmental regulations,[1] which can result in intergovernmental conflict. All of these issues can benefit from state-tribal collaboration. Moreover, a basic understanding of the legal framework and regulatory authority surrounding hunting and fishing activities and Indian water rights is provided to facilitate intergovernmental cooperation in these areas as well. Understanding the jurisdictional powers and constraints of each government can help policymakers identify areas that would benefit from state-tribal collaboration and allow conflicts to be readily addressed as issues arise. These policy topics are complex, and an in-depth discussion is beyond the scope of this publication. However, this chapter seeks to provide a brief overview of the regulatory scheme in each area for policymakers unfamiliar with these issues. It also seeks to provide a starting point for further inquiry and introduce areas prone to conflict so policymakers can determine what collaborative efforts exist in their community and spark ideas for additional collaboration.

As states and tribes engage in collaborative efforts around environmental regulation, it is important for policymakers to bear in mind the important role land, water, and other natural resources play in the lives of many Native Americans and Alaska Natives. Strongly held beliefs that the land and resources are sacred cause environmental regulation to become more than a policy issue—environmental harm is likely to be perceived as a threat to tribal culture and way of life. Policy solutions can be structured to respect these beliefs and address local priorities. In addition, state and tribal policymakers must balance economic development and community growth with environmental protection. As demand for scarce resources continues to grow, cooperation and creative solutions will be needed to advance the best interests and quality of life of both tribal and nontribal communities now and in the future.

MAJOR ENVIRONMENTAL LAWS, EPA INDIAN POLICY, AND TREATMENT AS STATE STATUS

Congress has enacted a number of statutes intended to protect the environment and control pollution. State and tribal governments are responsible for complying with federal environmental laws, and the U.S. Environmental Protection Agency (EPA) is typically responsible for administering these statutes. "The federal statutes establish minimum standards to be applied nationwide and encourage states to seek 'primacy' or primary regulatory authority to implement federal programs within their borders."[2]

The EPA Indian policy, originally issued in 1984 and reaffirmed in January 2014, recognizes tribal governments' authority for making decisions and carrying out program responsibilities affecting reservation communities, their environments, and the health and welfare of the reservation population.[3] Several federal environmental laws authorize the EPA to treat eligible tribes in the same manner as a state (TAS status) for purposes of implementing and managing certain environmental programs. These statutes include the Clean Air Act, the Clean Water Act, the

Safe Drinking Water Act, the Toxic Substance Control Act, and the Federal Insecticide, Fungicide and Rodenticide Act.[4] Other environmental statutes include provisions or were amended to treat tribes and states substantially similar without a requirement that tribes seek "state" status.[5]

In order to obtain treatment as state status, tribes must apply to the EPA and meet certain criteria. Generally speaking, a tribe is required to demonstrate that it is federally recognized, its governing body exercises substantial governmental powers, and it is reasonably capable of carrying out the functions it seeks to administer.[6] Tribes are also required to demonstrate jurisdictional authority over the area in question, though the requirements differ substantially under the major environmental statutes.[7] If a tribe or state does not assume primary regulatory responsibilities under the federal environmental statutes, the EPA will implement the regulatory requirements.[8]

As a general principle, states may not exercise jurisdiction over Indians on tribal land unless specifically authorized by Congress to do so. Federal Indian policy encourages tribal self-government in environmental matters, and nothing in the federal environmental statutes confers regulatory authority upon the states.[9] The authority of tribes over non-Indians in Indian country is limited, however. In order for tribes to regulate the conduct of non-Indians in Indian country the tribe must demonstrate an express congressional delegation of such authority or the presence of a *Montana* exception—meaning the non-Indian has entered into a consensual relationship with the tribe or its members or the non-Indian's conduct threatens or has some direct effect on the political integrity, economic security, or the health and welfare of the tribe.[10] (A broader discussion of the *Montana* exceptions and subsequent rulings further interpreting them is included in the *Civil Jurisdiction* chapter of this publication.) The potential impact of the regulated activity on the tribe must be serious and substantial. The harms that the various federal environmental statutes seek to address, however, are sufficiently serious that, if violated, they will likely satisfy the second *Montana* exception justifying tribal regulatory authority over non-Indians. Indeed, "[t]ribes generally rely on the 'health and welfare' exception to assert jurisdiction over non-members within the environmental sphere."[11] When necessary, the EPA will provide primary criminal enforcement of the federal environmental statutes within tribal jurisdictions (i.e., in relation to non-Indians) to the extent that a tribe is precluded from doing so.[12]

Given the jurisdictional limitations and uncertainty that can exist, intergovernmental cooperation can maximize the effectiveness of environmental policies and ensure that non-Indian land and non-Indians in Indian country are properly regulated. Moreover, the EPA Indian policy encourages communication and cooperation among state and tribal government that results in comprehensive planning and environmental management.[13] To be most effective environmental policies should be coordinated, as neighboring governments can achieve more by working together than either could acting alone.

The Southern Ute Indian/State of Colorado Environmental Commission Agreement Concerning Air Quality is an example of a cooperative effort that allowed the tribe and state to move beyond jurisdictional disputes and collaborate on environmental policies. The state and tribe reached an agreement to establish a single collaborative authority to promulgate rules and regulations for the reservation air quality program.[14] This was in response to a long-standing disagreement between the parties over who had regulatory authority over non-Indian-owned land within the Southern Ute reservation for purposes of administering the air quality control program under the Clean Air Act. Authorization for the agreement was provided by the Colorado legislature and the Southern Ute Tribal Council and was signed by the Colorado governor.[15] Although some disagreements as to jurisdictional authority remain, the focus of the collaboration is instead on how to best regulate air quality in the checkerboarded area.[16] Originally established in 1999, the Commission meets regularly with the purpose of overseeing the development and implementation of a comprehensive air quality protection program throughout the Southern Ute reservation.[17]

REGULATION OF HUNTING AND FISHING

Tribal Regulatory Authority

Tribes have inherent authority, as a function of their sovereignty, to regulate their land and the conduct of their members. This includes the power to regulate hunting and fishing on tribal land.[18] The tribe's regulatory authority generally extends to nonmembers hunting or fishing on tribal land unless, perhaps, the state can identify an off-reservation effect or state interest that justifies the assertion of concurrent regulatory authority (state and tribe may both exercise jurisdiction) over nonmembers on tribal land.[19] Individuals who hunt or fish on tribal land without the permission of the tribe are subject to punishment under federal law.[20]

In order to regulate the hunting and fishing activities of non-Indians on non-Indian land within the reservation, the tribe must demonstrate that the non-Indian has entered into a consensual relationship with the tribe or the non-Indian conduct threatens the tribe's political integrity, economic security, or health and welfare, in accordance with *Montana v. United States*.[21] As indicated by several Supreme Court decisions, if the tribe is unable to demonstrate these circumstances, the conduct of non-Indians will be subject to state regulation.

State Regulatory Authority

States are not authorized to regulate a tribal member's federal hunting and fishing rights on state land, nor do states have authority to regulate tribal members hunting and fishing on tribal land, even in states subject to Public Law 280.[22] The limitation stems from the premise that states are prohibited from exercising state law on tribal land whenever the application of state law infringes upon a tribe's right to be self-governing or is preempted by federal law.[23] (A broader discussion of the "infringement" and "preemption" tests can be found in the *Civil Jurisdiction* chapter of this publication.) There is an exception to this rule, however, established in the Supreme Court case of *Puyallup Tribe v. Department of Game*.[24] In this case the court ruled that a state may regulate the exercise of Indian treaty rights (both on the reservation and off) when necessary for conservation purposes[25] provided the state regulation is reasonable and necessary to perpetuate the species, the regulation is the least restrictive means of achieving the conservation goal, no alternative methods of conservation that are less harmful to the tribe's rights are available, and the regulation does not discriminate against Indians.[26]

States may regulate hunting and fishing by tribal members outside the reservation not pursuant to federal treaty rights in the same manner as the state regulates any other state citizen.

INDIAN WATER RIGHTS

Indian water rights were defined in the 1908 Supreme Court case of *Winters v. United States*.[27] In this case the court ruled that when the United States sets aside land for Indians, such as through the establishment of reservations, water rights are reserved by implication. As such, Indian water rights have become known as *Winters* rights and differ from non-Indian riparian or appropriative water rights.

Riparian rights apply to states in the eastern United States in which water tends to be readily available. Under this system a landowner has the right to reasonable use of water existing on the property, and these rights are not lost through nonuse. The right to the water runs with the land and cannot be separated. If water becomes scarce, the rights of each riparian owner are diminished proportionally.[28] Appropriative rights generally apply to states in the western United States in which water is more scarce. These rights belong to the first user who appropriates the water and puts it to beneficial use. This right is guaranteed to continue as long as the beneficial use continues. These rights do not run with the land and are transferable. If the water supply becomes scarce, the initial appropriator has the right to their entire share, even though the rights of later appropriators may be lost or diminished. As a result, appropriation dates are extremely important in determining the seniority of rights.[29]

Indian water rights, or *Winters* rights, are created and governed by federal law.[30] A tribe cannot lose its *Winters* rights through nonuse, and the amount of water a tribe is entitled to use is not determined or limited by the tribe's initial use.[31] Indian water rights are deemed reserved as of the time the reservation was established in an amount sufficient to make the land habitable and productive.[32] Competing users with earlier appropriation dates will have seniority, though "[m]ost Indian reservations in the West were created before non-Indians acquired much or any land in the region. As a result, Indian water rights usually have an early priority date, and thus they are particularly valuable."[33] The United States holds legal title to *Winters* rights as trustee for the tribes. As such, the United States is an indispensable party to any adjudication of those rights. Historically these disputes have been heard in federal court, though the Supreme Court has ruled that Congress waived the sovereign immunity of the United States via the McCarran Amendment in 1952, making adjudication in state court possible as well.[34]

An attribute of Indian water rights that often leads to conflict is the fact that these rights are not specifically quantified and, until relatively recently, most tribes did not make significant use of their rights. The Supreme Court ruled in the case of *Arizona v. California*[35] that tribes are entitled to enough water to irrigate all the practicably irrigable acreage on the reservation, and subsequent court decisions have recognized the need to be flexible regarding the tribes' use of water for a variety of purposes to promote self-sufficiency.[36] As tribes begin to assert their water rights, conflict and litigation between the state and tribal governments have resulted.

> Non-Indians contend that recognition of long-dormant Indian rights defeats the entire purpose of the appropriative systems, which was to create certainty that would stimulate beneficial use. . . . The tribes contend, however, that the reason for their non-use of the water was the failure of the United States to fulfill its responsibility as trustee in developing and protecting water resources, and that it would only compound injury to deprive the tribes of their water forever.[37]

Litigation and surveys to determine irrigability are time-consuming and costly. As with many other policy challenges facing states and tribes, communication and cooperation are likely to produce better long-term results for everyone involved. "[T]he hard reality is that years-long litigation over water rights works to no party's benefit, exacts enormous financial costs and creates further obstacles to long-range economic planning and development."[38] For these reasons, states and tribes have begun to quantify Indian water rights by negotiation, administrative action, or legislation, and negotiated settlements are increasingly common.[39] For example, the Reserved Water Rights Compact Commission (RWRCC) in Montana was created by the state's legislature in 1979 as part of a statewide general stream adjudication process to negotiate settlements with the tribes and federal agencies claiming reserved water rights in Montana.[40] Since the passage of the Montana Water Use Act of 1973, an adjudication process has been under way to finalize all water rights prior to the passage of this act. As part of these negotiations, the RWWCC and the federal agency holding the water rights must quantify the rights in accordance with the purpose for which the federal reservation was created. (In Montana reserved water rights have been claimed for Indian reservations as well as for national parks, forests, wildlife refuges, and federally designated wild and scenic rivers within the state.) Seventeen compacts have been negotiated and approved by the legislature between the RWWCC and six Montana tribes since 1979.[41]

As population growth, new economic ventures, and the effects of climate change all place increasing demands on water resources, intergovernmental cooperation and ongoing communication can help resolve conflicts without litigation and ensure the needs of all citizens are met.

9

NATIVE AMERICAN GRAVES PROTECTION AND REPATRIATION ACT

The Native American Graves Protection and Repatriation Act (NAGPRA) is a federal law that was enacted on November 16, 1990. The purpose of the Act is to provide protection for Native American burial sites and to establish a process for the repatriation—or return—of Native American human remains and cultural items, specifically funerary and sacred objects, and objects of cultural patrimony, housed in museum or institutional collections. The Act applies to federally recognized Indian tribes and Alaska Native villages (which are included within the definition of Indian tribes for purposes of NAGPRA), and Native Hawaiian organizations (NHO). The Secretary of the Interior oversees NAGPRA, and the national NAGPRA program is located within the National Park Service (NPS).

NAGPRA was intended to end the practice of removing Native American human remains and cultural objects for incorporation into museum collections without the consent of lineal descendants or culturally affiliated tribes. Given the cultural significance of death and burial rights for many Native Americans, at the time of its passage "NAGPRA was hailed as a significant landmark in civil rights, human rights, and Indian law."[1] NAGPRA governs the handling and treatment of both human remains and cultural items in collections and those items on federal or tribal land. Human remains and cultural items on state or private land are not governed by the Act, though many states have enacted legislation similar to NAGPRA to protect burial sites in these areas. Consultation with tribes is required under NAGPRA, and it will also be necessary (or at least beneficial) under most state burial site protection laws. This chapter provides an overview of NAGPRA's requirements so policymakers can identify areas in which state action and/or state-tribal cooperation is needed to ensure state compliance and facilitate the purpose of the Act.

HUMAN REMAINS AND CULTURAL ITEMS IN COLLECTIONS

The provisions of NAGPRA governing human remains and cultural items in collections are broad in their applicability. All federal agencies are subject to NAGPRA as well as any museum that receives federal funds. This includes any institution, state or local government agency, and colleges and universities that receive federal funds and have possession or control over Native American cultural items with the exception of the Smithsonian Institution,[2] which is governed by the National Museum of the American Indian Act of 1989. Failure to comply with NAGPRA's requirements can result in civil penalties.

NAGPRA's repatriation process requires federal agencies and museums to identify items in their collections that are subject to NAGPRA and prepare an inventory of these items. Consultation with lineal descendants, Indian tribes, and NHOs is required regarding the identification and cultural affiliation of items included in the collection inventories, and federal agencies and museums must provide notice that the cultural items may be repatriated.[3] The Secretary of the Interior is required to publish these notices in the Federal Register. NAGPRA does not require consultation regarding repatriation with tribes that are not federally recognized, though museums may choose to do so in instances in which non–federally recognized tribes are believed to be the appropriate claimant for cultural items.[4]

It is unclear exactly how many Native American remains or cultural items have been repatriated since NAGPRA was passed in 1990, as there is no requirement that federal agencies or museums report repatriations to the Secretary of the Interior or the National Park Service.[5] However, notices of items published in the Federal Register provide figures on the total number of human remains and cultural items that are eligible for repatriation on an annual basis. For example, as of September 30, 2014, notices were published in the Federal Register for 50,158 individual human remains, 1,185,948 associated funerary objects (including small items such as beads), 219,956 unassociated funerary objects, 4,914 sacred objects, 8,118 objects of cultural patrimony, and 1,624 objects that are both sacred and patrimonial.[6]

Difficulties have arisen in regard to the repatriation of human remains and cultural items that have been determined to be Native American but cannot be culturally affiliated with a tribe or NHO. These items are referred to as culturally unidentifiable (CUI). Concerns have been voiced that unaffiliated objects, in some instances, are actually affiliated, and museums have declared them unidentifiable as a way of retaining items in their collections for further study. New regulations went into effect in 2010, however, regarding the disposition of CUIs in order to facilitate repatriation to the appropriate tribe or NHO. These regulations require federal agencies and museums to initiate consultation on CUIs within 90 days of a request to transfer control of a CUI from a tribe(s) or NHO(s) from whose tribal lands or aboriginal territory the remains were exhumed.[7] If cultural affiliation is made possible as a result of the consultation, federal agencies and museums must comply with federal notification and repatriation requirements.[8]

HUMAN REMAINS AND CULTURAL ITEMS ON TRIBAL AND FEDERAL LAND

NAGPRA establishes a process for determining ownership and the return of human remains and cultural items found on federal or tribal land after November 16, 1990. For purposes of the Act, tribal land includes all land within the exterior boundaries of any Indian reservation (including privately owned land), all dependent Indian communities, and any lands administered for the benefit of Native Hawaiians pursuant to the Native Hawaiians Homes Commission Act and the Hawaii Statehood Admissions Act.[9] If the human remains or cultural items are found on state or private land, NAGPRA does not apply, but other federal cultural preservation laws or state or local laws may be applicable.[10]

Ownership. Native American human remains and associated funerary objects (those objects placed with the human remains at or following the time of death) belong to the lineal descendant(s) of the deceased individual.[11] If no lineal descendant can be determined, the human remains and associated funerary objects belong to the tribe or NHO on whose tribal land such objects or remains were discovered or with the closest culturally affiliated tribe or NHO that makes a claim.[12] If cultural affiliation cannot be determined, ownership lies with the tribe recognized as aboriginally occupying the land where the remains and objects were discovered and who, upon notice, makes a claim.[13] The ownership claim by the tribe recognized as aboriginally occupying the land where the remains and objects were found can be preempted by another tribe making a claim of ownership if demonstrated that the tribe has a stronger cultural connection to the remains or objects than the aboriginal tribe.[14] Priority of ownership claims of sacred objects, objects of cultural patrimony, and unassociated funerary objects (those objects used as part of the death rite or ceremony and believed to have been placed with human remains at or following the time of death but are no longer associated or found with human remains) follows the same order of tribe/NHO ownership priority as that discussed above.

Excavation and Discovery. NAGPRA also establishes a process governing the excavation or discovery of Native American human remains and cultural objects found on federal or tribal land. NAGPRA permits intentional excavation of Native American human remains and cultural items on tribal land if the appropriate Indian tribe or NHO has given consent and a permit, issued pursuant to the Archaeological Resources Protection Act (ARPA), has been obtained.[15] Intentional excavation on federal land requires that the appropriate federal agency provide written notification to and engage in consultation with any known lineal descendants and the appropriate Indian tribe or NHO who are likely to have a cultural relationship or affiliation with the human remains and items expected to be found and tribes or NHOs on whose aboriginal lands the excavation will take place.[16] The consultation is intended to help the federal agency determine ownership of the human remains and/or cultural objects, in accordance with NAGPRA ownership priorities, and to discuss the federal agency's proposed treatment of the human remains and other items.[17] Consultation must be followed by a written plan of action detailing the planned treatment, care, and handling of the cultural items, the kinds of analysis planned for each kind of object, and the nature of any reports to be prepared.[18] Before final disposition of the remains or cultural items can occur, the federal agency must provide notice of the disposition published twice in a newspaper of general circulation in the area in which the remains and cultural items were found and in the area(s) in which members of the affiliated tribe or NHO now reside.[19]

Any person who makes an inadvertent discovery of Native American remains or cultural objects must notify the appropriate federal officials. If the discovery occurs in connection with an ongoing activity (such as construction, agriculture, mining, etc.), the activity must cease and reasonable efforts must be made to protect the remains and other items. The appropriate federal official must initiate consultation with any known lineal descendants and the appropriate Indian tribe or NHO who are likely to have a cultural relationship or affiliation with the human remains and items found and tribes or NHOs on whose aboriginal lands the items were discovered.[20] As with consultation regarding excavation activities, consultation regarding inadvertent discoveries are intended to help the federal agency determine ownership and to communicate the federal agency's proposed treatment of the remains and cultural items.[21] This includes a determination as to whether the discovered items will be left in place. If so, the federal agency is responsible for securing the site of discovery and no further action is taken. If the items are to be removed, excavation must be conducted in accordance with the ARPA.[22] Requirements for written plans of action and notice and publication requirements prior to disposition are the same for inadvertent discoveries as for excavation.

STATE BURIAL SITE PROTECTION LAWS

Many states have enacted legislation similar to NAGPRA that provides burial site protection on state or private land. For example, California has incorporated NAGPRA's requirements into state law, extending protection to all nonfederal public and private property in the state.[23] California's law expands NAGPRA's scope, however, by providing a mechanism whereby tribes that are not federally recognized may file repatriation claims.[24]

Louisiana enacted the Unmarked Human Burial Sites Preservation Act shortly after the passage of NAGPRA to provide protection of unmarked burial sites in response to concerns that economic development activities could pose a threat to the integrity of prehistoric and historic Indian, pioneer, and Civil War and other soldiers' burial sites.[25] This law is broader in scope than California's law in that it is not limited to protection of Native American burial sites but is intended to "protect human burials 'without reference to ethnic origins, cultural backgrounds, or religious affiliation' and to ensure 'proper archaeological investigation' when disturbance of such sites is unavoidable."[26] In addition, Louisiana's law requires consultation with descendant groups in regard to the disposition of any human remains that have been disturbed intentionally, unintentionally, or by permit.[27] In cases in which no descendant group can be identified or fails to take responsibility, the state makes determinations regarding disposition of the remains.[28]

In Colorado, extensive collaboration between History Colorado (HC), a state agency that receives federal funding, the Colorado Commission of Indian Affairs (CCIA), and the tribes located in the state resulted in a number of positive outcomes that support compliance with NAGPRA and provide protection for Native American human remains and cultural objects discovered on state and private land. "To address ongoing interagency responsibilities regarding NAGPRA, including discoveries on state and private lands, HC established the shared position of NAGPRA liaison in November 1998 through an NPS NAGPRA grant partnership with CCIA."[29] In response to tribal concerns that it was taking too long to rebury individuals who had been disinterred, CCIA developed a reinterment committee, also in 1998, focused on NAGPRA consultations with HC and tribes, rewriting the state's burial law and developing a statewide reburial plan.[30] In 2000, HC and CCIA partnered on an NPS NAGPRA grant to hold a symposium focused on NAGPRA's cultural affiliation standard, providing HC with additional clarification needed to culturally affiliate many individuals previously designated as culturally unidentifiable under NAGPRA.[31] In addition, HC and CCIA developed a process, approved by the Department of the Interior in 2008 prior to the promulgation of 43 CFR §10.11 in 2010 (regarding disposition of culturally unidentifiable remains), governing the disposition of culturally unidentifiable human remains and funerary objects.[32] A key requirement associated with this process is the establishment of timelines HC agreed to follow to ensure that CUI remains are not held indefinitely.[33] Since the promulgation of the federal regulations governing CUIs, it has been determined that the Colorado process goes beyond the federal requirements and poses no conflict with federal law.[34]

A number of lessons learned from HC's tribal consultations may be useful to policymakers in other areas. These include:[35]

- Working with tribes from the beginning to collaboratively develop goals and agenda items for consultation meetings;
- Ensuring that consultation meetings allow a dialogue among participants;
- Use of facilitators during consultation meetings to help establish guiding principles for respectful communication that allows for the expression of all ideas;
- Transparency and consistency in the process;
- Development of written policies as appropriate.

Finally, there is a belief at HC that many positive outcomes have resulted from the agency's efforts to comply with NAGPRA's requirements. These include improved staff knowledge of the agency's collections, tribal partnerships that transcend NAGPRA, enhanced interpretation in exhibits and education programs, and, perhaps most importantly, an improved ability to convey to the agency's audience what Native American community members want others to understand about them.[36]

10

THE INDIAN CHILD WELFARE ACT

The Indian Child Welfare Act (ICWA) was enacted by Congress in 1978 to provide for tribal jurisdiction over child custody proceedings involving Indian children. The Act recognizes that, in furtherance of the federal trust responsibility, the U.S. government has an obligation to protect Indian tribes and their resources, and no resource is more vital to the continued existence of the tribes than Indian children.[1]

The law's enactment was prompted by nationwide studies by the Association of American Indian Affairs conducted between 1969 and 1974 that revealed 25 percent to 35 percent of Indian children were being removed from their homes and placed in non-Indian foster or adoptive homes by state courts and state child welfare agencies. Indian children were removed from their homes at a much higher rate than non-Indian children due, in part, to a failure of state officials to understand the important role that cultural beliefs, extended family, and connections to the tribe play in the life of Indian children. In addition, high rates of alcoholism and poverty—a by-product of the detrimental federal Indian policies of the past—were relied on as justifications for removing Indian children from their communities. Very few Indian children were being removed from their families due to physical abuse.[2] "The wholesale separation of Indian children from their families [was] perhaps the most tragic and destructive aspect of American Indian life" of the day.[3] This alarming rate of removal was so extreme, it came to be viewed as a form of cultural genocide. ICWA was intended to address these problems by affirming tribal authority over Indian child welfare cases and to help ensure that actions taken by state officials are not guided by cultural bias and misunderstanding but instead, truly serve the best interests of Indian children.

ICWA is a federal law, and states are required to abide by it. Unfortunately, state officials often are uninformed about the Act and fail to effectively implement it. State compliance with the Act remains vitally important, both to prevent the damage done by the alarming rate of out-of-home placements of the past and to promote good outcomes that uphold the goals of the Act in cases moving forward.

> Studies examining the long-term outcomes for Native American adults who were adopted as children find increased rates of depression, low self-esteem, and suicide, despite socioeconomic advantages that many experienced in their adoptive home relative to their homes of origin. Many of these adult adoptees continue to experience identity issues and report feelings of isolation and loneliness. Today, Native American children are still more than twice as likely as non-Indian children to be placed in foster care.[4]

As a result, state compliance with ICWA is essential to ensuring that Indian child welfare cases are handled appropriately, promoting the well-being of Indian children and healthy tribal communities.

OVERVIEW OF THE ACT

The overarching purpose of the Indian Child Welfare Act has two main components:[5]

- To protect the best interests of Indian children and promote stability and security of Indian tribes and families by the establishment of minimum federal standards for the removal of Indian children from their families and the placement of such children in foster or adoptive homes which will reflect the unique values of Indian culture, and
- To provide assistance to Indian tribes in the operation of child and family services programs.

The discussion below is designed to provide state policymakers with a working understanding of key provisions of the Act so that areas for improved ICWA compliance can be identified, steps can be taken to ensure proper ICWA enforcement by state courts and child welfare agencies, and so that state and tribal policymakers can determine where ongoing cooperation may be needed to ensure that the goals of the Act are upheld.

APPLICABILITY OF THE ACT

ICWA applies to child custody proceedings including foster care placement, termination of parental rights, preadoptive placements, and adoptive placements involving an unmarried individual under the age of eighteen who is a member of or is eligible for membership in a federally recognized Indian tribe or Alaska Native village. Membership status and eligibility is defined by the child's tribe, and the state is prohibited from making such determinations.[6] The Act also applies to juvenile delinquency proceedings if the proceeding results in the child's placement in foster care, preadoptive or adoptive placement, or a termination of parental rights.

ICWA does not apply to divorce or custody proceedings in which an award of custody is made to one of the parents, voluntary placements of the child in which a parent is not prohibited from regaining custody upon demand, or to tribal court proceedings.

JURISDICTIONAL AUTHORITY

The allocation of jurisdictional authority under ICWA is fundamental to the goals and overarching purpose of the Act—to protect the best interests of Indian children and to promote the stability and security of Indian tribes and Indian families. The Act recognizes a tribe's authority over child custody proceedings for children domiciled on the reservation and over children who are wards of the tribal court, regardless of whether they are domiciled on or off the reservation. In such instances the tribe has exclusive jurisdiction, unless jurisdiction has been granted to the state via federal law, such as Public Law 83-280 (P.L. 280).[7] Any orders issued by the tribal court in regard to Indian child custody proceedings must be given full faith and credit.[8]

The Act provides for concurrent, but presumptively tribal, jurisdiction over state court proceedings involving Indian children who are not domiciled on the reservation. In such cases the state court must transfer the case to the tribal court upon the request of the child's tribe, the child's parent, or the child's Indian custodian unless good cause not to transfer the case to tribal court has been demonstrated. A transfer of jurisdiction to the tribal court can also be prevented based on an objection from either of the child's parents. The presumption of tribal jurisdiction over cases originating in state court is intended to protect the rights of the Indian child but also the rights of the child's tribe. In regard to Indian child welfare cases remaining in the state court system, the Indian custodian and the child's tribe have a right to intervene at any time.[9]

States are permitted to exercise jurisdiction over an Indian child in emergency situations in which it is necessary to remove the child from his or her parent(s) and place the child in a foster home or institution in order to prevent imminent physical damage or harm to the child. The state's authority under this provision of ICWA is temporary, and the emergency placement must be terminated once it is no longer necessary. The state must then initiate a child custody proceeding pursuant to ICWA, transfer jurisdiction of the matter to the appropriate tribe, or return the child to the custody of his or her parent(s) or Indian custodian, as appropriate under the circumstances.[10]

DOMICILE

The Indian child's domicile determines whether tribes have exclusive jurisdiction (in non–P.L. 280 states) or whether jurisdiction is concurrent with the state. ICWA does not provide a definition of domicile, though the Supreme Court has ruled that, for purposes of determining jurisdiction, Congress intended a uniform definition of domicile, as it pertains to ICWA, unaffected by state-law definitions.[11] As such, the court has clarified that the domicile of the child will be the same as the domicile of the mother.[12]

NOTICE REQUIREMENTS

The child's parents or Indian custodian and the child's tribe are entitled to notice of any state court child custody proceeding involving an Indian child. The party seeking foster care placement or termination of parental rights must provide notice of the pending proceeding and the right to intervene. If identification of or contact with the child's parent, Indian custodian, and tribe cannot be made, notice must be provided to the Secretary of the Interior, who will then have 15 days to provide notice to the parent or Indian custodian and the tribe.[13] If the court has any reason to believe, but has been unable to confirm, that the child involved in the custody proceeding is an Indian child, the state court must abide by the requirements of ICWA until it is determined that the child is not an Indian child subject to the Act.[14]

EFFORTS TO PREVENT BREAKUP OF THE INDIAN FAMILY

In order to prevent hasty decisions about out-of-home placements of Indian children based on cultural bias or lack of understanding of the tribal community, ICWA requires state courts or child welfare agencies to demonstrate that active efforts have been made to provide remedial or rehabilitative services to prevent the breakup of the Indian family and alleviate the need for foster or adoptive placements.

If the efforts to prevent the breakup of the family prove unsuccessful, orders for foster care placement must be supported by clear and convincing evidence, including supporting testimony by qualified expert witnesses, that the parent's continued custody of the child will likely result in serious emotional or physical damage to the child.[15] Orders for termination of parental rights require that an even higher evidentiary standard be met. These orders must be supported by evidence beyond a reasonable doubt, including supporting testimony by qualified expert witnesses, that the parent's continued custody of the child is likely to result in serious emotional or physical damage to the child.[16]

PLACEMENT PREFERENCES

Placement preferences are set forth in ICWA that apply to both foster care and preadoptive and adoptive placements. State courts handling ICWA cases must comply with the placement preferences, unless there is good cause to do otherwise. In foster care and preadoptive placements, preference must be given to (1) a member of the child's extended family, (2) a foster home licensed, approved, or specified by the Indian child's tribe, (3) an Indian foster home licensed or approved by an authorized non-Indian licensing authority, or (4) an institution for children approved by the tribe or operated by an Indian organization which has a program suitable to meet the needs of the Indian child who is the subject of the proceeding.[17] In adoptive placements, preference must be given to (1) a member of the child's extended family, (2) other members of the child's tribe, or (3) other Indian families.[18]

In instances in which the child's tribe has established a different order of preference than that specified in the Act, the state court or agency handling the case must abide by the tribe's placement preferences.[19]

RESUMPTION OF TRIBAL JURISDICTION IN P.L. 280 STATES

Tribes that are subject to state jurisdiction pursuant to P.L. 280 or any other federal law may petition the Secretary of the Interior to reassume jurisdiction over child custody proceedings involving Indian children.[20]

STATE-TRIBAL AGREEMENTS

ICWA explicitly authorizes agreements among the states and tribes that further clarify and address jurisdiction and handling of child custody proceedings involving Indian children.[21] Indeed, a number of such agreements exist, and many states have enacted state legislation intended to increase compliance with the Act. In instances in which state law provides a higher standard of protection of the rights of the parent or Indian custodian than protections provide under ICWA, state courts are required to apply the higher standard.[22]

BIA GUIDELINES

A number of ambiguities in ICWA can cause uncertainty in its implementation at the state level. These include lack of clarity over the requirement that "active efforts" must be made to prevent the breakup of the Indian family; what constitutes "good cause" for deviating from the foster care and adoptive placement preferences or declining to transfer a case to the tribal court; and what skills or experience are needed so that an individual may serve as a "qualified expert witness" testifying to the need for foster care placement or the appropriateness of the termination of parental rights.

In February 2015, the Bureau of Indian Affairs issued updated *Guidelines for State Courts and Agencies in Indian Child Custody Proceedings*[23] in an effort to provide more certainty surrounding some of the more ambiguous provisions of ICWA. The *Guidelines* specify that "active efforts" to provide remedial services and connect families with rehabilitative programs designed to prevent the breakup of the family require heightened efforts, beyond what is required under the Title IV-E Federal Foster Care Program. Efforts should be focused on maintaining the family unit or reunifying the child with his or her family or tribal community and include:[24]

- Engaging the child, the child's parents, extended family, and custodians
- Taking steps necessary to keep siblings together
- Identifying appropriate services and helping the parents overcome barriers, including actively assisting the parents in obtaining such services
- Identifying, notifying, and inviting representatives of the Indian child's tribe to participate
- Conducting a diligent search for the Indian child's extended family members for assistance and possible placements
- Taking into account the child's tribe's prevailing social and cultural standards
- Offering and employing all available and culturally appropriate family preservation strategies

- Completing a comprehensive assessment of the circumstances of the child's family, with a focus on safe reunification as the most desirable goal
- Notifying and consulting with extended family members of the child to provide family structure and support for the child, to assure cultural connections, and to serve as placement resources for the child
- Making arrangements to provide family interaction in the most natural setting that can ensure the child's safety during any necessary removal
- Identifying community resources including housing, financial, transportation, mental health, substance abuse, and peer support services and actively assisting the child's parents and extended family in utilizing or accessing those resources
- Monitoring progress and participation in services
- Providing consideration of alternative ways of addressing the needs of the child's parents and extended family, if services do not exist, or if existing services are not available
- Supporting regular visits and trial home visits of the child during any period of removal, consistent with the need to ensure the safety of the child
- Providing postreunification services and monitoring

Determinations that "good cause" exists to deviate from ICWA's placement preferences must be supported by clear and convincing evidence, and any party seeking to deviate from the preferences must state their reasons on the record or in writing. Good cause for noncompliance with the placement preferences must be based on the request of the parents, the request of the child (if the child is capable of understanding the decision under consideration), the extraordinary physical or emotional needs of the child, or the unavailability of a placement that complies with ICWA's preference structure, provided that the court determines that active efforts have been made to find a placement that conforms with the preference criteria and none were located.[25]

In determining whether "good cause" exists to retain the case in state court, the court may not consider whether the case is at an advanced stage or whether the transfer would result in a change in the child's placement. Assertions that good cause exists not to transfer the case to tribal court also must be made on the record or in writing. In addition, the *Guidelines* explicitly acknowledge a presumption that "whenever a parent or tribe seeks to transfer an Indian child custody case from state court to tribal court, it is presumptively in the best interest of the child, consistent with the Act, to transfer the case to the jurisdiction of the tribe."[26]

Finally, orders placing a child in foster care must be supported by clear and convincing evidence, and orders terminating parental rights must be supported by evidence beyond a reasonable doubt.[27] In each instance, the evidence should be supported, in part, by the testimony of "expert witnesses," though the Act itself does not define what skills and experience are needed to qualify as an expert. The *Guidelines* provide further clarification on this issue. First and foremost, a qualified expert must have specific knowledge of the tribe's culture and customs. Individuals who are presumed to qualify as experts include a member of the child's tribe recognized by the tribal community as having knowledge of tribal customs pertaining to family organization and child-rearing practices; a member of another tribe recognized as an expert by the child's tribe based on their knowledge of the delivery of child and family services to Indians generally and to the child's tribe; a layperson recognized by the tribe as having experience in the delivery of child and family services to Indians, and knowledge of cultural standards and child-rearing practices within the child's tribe; or a professional with demonstrated knowledge of cultural standards and child-rearing practices within the child's tribe.[28]

STATE ACTIVITY

Despite improvements that have occurred in the handling of Indian child welfare cases since the enactment of ICWA in 1978, consistent state compliance with the Act continues to be a problem. ICWA is most effective when a child's Indian identity is made known early in the proceedings, when the child's family and tribe receive timely notice that a child welfare proceeding involving a member or member-eligible child is pending in the state court system, and when state courts carefully follow the statutory mandates.[29]

Timely notice of a child's Indian status is a key factor in ensuring that ICWA cases are handled appropriately from the start, reducing the potential for the interests of the tribe and the interests of the child to come into conflict. For example, resistance toward the application of ICWA in the late stages of a case, when permanent placement decisions must be made, often stems from the failure to abide by the requirements of ICWA from the onset of circumstances giving rise to the case. Such was the situation in the controversial 2013 Supreme Court case of *Adoptive Couple v. Baby Girl*.[30] In these cases state courts may be resistant to comply with ICWA's placement preferences favoring placement with the child's extended family or an Indian custodian over placement with a non-Indian custodian when the child has remained in the care of a non-Indian custodian for a long period of time. Early identification of ICWA cases and strict compliance with the notice requirements can prevent similar problems in the future.

State policymakers and officials have employed a number of techniques to improve ICWA compliance and ensure that the goals and purpose of the Act are upheld. For example, the New Mexico Tribal-State Judicial Consortium developed an ICWA Judicial Bench Card that provides reference materials for tribal and state judges as they handle ICWA cases.[31] In other instances states have enacted their own Indian child welfare laws designed to explicitly require compliance with the federal Act or to further clarify policies and procedures for ICWA implementation. These efforts include specific definitions of what constitutes "active efforts" to prevent the breakup of the Indian family; expanded definitions of what constitutes the Indian child's extended family for foster care, preadoptive, and adoptive placements; and clarification regarding jurisdiction. Legislation or agency-level policies clarifying jurisdiction and the transfer of cases from state to tribal court can be particularly useful in states subject to P.L. 280.

In addition, states have enacted legislation designed to improve early identification of ICWA cases and improve notice of the proceedings to the child's family and tribe, so that questions regarding the appropriateness of placement decisions do not have to be reconsidered late in a case.

States may also find it useful to incorporate full faith and credit provisions in their statutes or ICWA-related legislation, explicitly acknowledging that tribal court orders pertaining to Indian child custody proceedings must be recognized by the state. Finally, requiring state-tribal consultation regarding foster care, preadoptive, and adoptive placements can improve outcomes for children, and cross-court consortiums can facilitate information sharing and identification of best practices.

FUNDING ISSUES

Funding to support the establishment and operation of Indian child welfare and family programs can be authorized by the Secretary of the Interior through a grant program established under ICWA. This funding is intended to support programs designed to prevent the breakup of the Indian family and prevent the child's removal from the custody of his or her parents.[32] Unfortunately, funding available under ICWA has been inadequate to support the full and effective implementation of the Act. As a result, tribes have had to look to other sources of funding beyond ICWA appropriations—primarily to programs administered by the Department of Health and Human Services.[33]

Title IV-E of the Social Security Act is the principal federal funding mechanism for foster care and adoption assistance programs, though it is only recently that tribes have been able to access this funding directly.[34] The Fostering Connections to Success and Increasing Adoptions Act of 2008 added a new section to the Social Security Act which allows tribes the option to apply for direct funding (as opposed to pass-through dollars channeled through the state) to support the administration of tribal foster care, adoption assistance, and guardianship assistance programs under Title IV-E of the Social Security Act. The Act also permits the continuation of existing state-tribal agreements or the establishment of new agreements in connection with operation of Title IV-E programs.[35] State legislation has been enacted in some areas to address the negotiation of state-tribal agreements and cooperative efforts around Title IV-E foster care programs. Policymakers may find it useful to support increased collaboration around this issue so that programs can be made as effective as possible and scarce resources can be maximized and targeted more efficiently.

11

HUMAN SERVICES

The need for cooperation between states and tribes has increased significantly in the area of human services due to the devolution of federal funding, program administration, and service delivery to the state and tribal governments. Devolution has occurred with a number of human services programs including welfare reform, child support enforcement, and education-related partnerships, and is driven by the belief that state and tribal policymakers (as opposed to federal officials) are in a position to most accurately assess the unique needs that exist in their communities. Block grant funding and program flexibility capitalize on local knowledge and make it possible for policymakers to craft programs that effectively address their unique needs. The flexibility afforded through the devolution of federal human services programs also allows for creative partnerships between state and tribal government so challenges experienced among neighboring or overlapping citizenry can be handled collaboratively, maximizing resources and opportunities. This chapter provides an overview of the Temporary Assistance to Needy Families (TANF) program, the Child Support Enforcement program, and the State-Tribal Education Partnership to highlight the growing body of intergovernmental collaboration that exists in these areas and to help policymakers identify and consider areas for future cooperation.

TEMPORARY ASSISTANCE TO NEEDY FAMILIES

The Personal Responsibility and Work Opportunity Reconciliation Act of 1996 (PRWORA) is a block grant program that authorized states and tribes to administer their own Temporary Assistance to Needy Families (welfare) programs. Decision-making authority regarding program expenditures and responsibility for program administration was devolved to the state and tribal governments. Policymakers are afforded flexibility in their funding allocation decisions so long as the expenditures support program activities that further the purpose of the program. The purpose of the TANF program is (1) to provide assistance to needy families so that children can be cared for in their own homes; (2) to reduce the dependency of needy parents by promoting job preparation, work, and marriage; (3) to prevent and reduce the incidence of out-of-wedlock pregnancies; and (4) to encourage the formation and maintenance of two-parent families.[1] In the years since the enactment of PRWORA, the number of tribal TANF programs has been growing. As of January 1, 2015, there were 70 approved tribal TANF programs serving 284 federally recognized tribes and Alaska Native villages.[2]

Program participants are required to engage in work activities in order to receive cash assistance but also receive various other support services to help parents find and maintain employment. State and tribal governments have authority to determine program eligibility criteria, set benefit levels, and make other determinations regarding program rules and regulations within the parameters set forth under the federal statute. In order to operate a TANF program, tribes are required to submit a three-year plan to the Secretary of the Department of Health and Human Services (DHHS) through the Administration for Children and Families for review and approval. If approved, the tribal TANF program receives a portion of the state TANF block grant from the state in which the tribe is located.[3] In order to receive federal block grant funding, states are required to make financial contributions to their programs. This provision is referred to as maintenance of effort (MOE) and requires states to maintain a significant portion of their historic funding levels to their welfare programs. Although states are not required to provide funding to tribal TANF programs, many do, and this funding counts toward the state's MOE requirement.[4]

While states and tribes are both afforded flexibility in program funding choices and design, the federal requirements for state and tribal programs differ in some respects, mainly in the areas of block grant amounts, allowable expenditures for administrative costs, the scope of allowable work activities, work participation rates, time limits on receipt of cash assistance, and determinations regarding hardship exemptions.[5] The additional flexibility afforded to tribes is intended to ensure that tribal TANF programs are responsive to local needs and specific challenges within the tribal community.

For example, tribes have authority to define the service area and population to be served under the tribal TANF program including whether the program will serve other Indian families residing in the community, or be limited to tribal members. Tribes have broader authority to define what types of activities will satisfy the work participation requirements for program participants. Tribes can set their own work participation rates, work hour requirements, and time limits on the receipt of cash assistance. Tribes also have flexibility to determine the scope of time limit exemptions based on hardship or other specific circumstances, subject to DHHS approval.[6]

A 2011 report by the Government Accountability Office examined how tribal TANF programs have changed over the last several years and how these programs weathered the economic downturn that began in 2007. Findings from this review indicate that tribal TANF programs experience ongoing problems associated with program implementation, staff development and retention, and development of adequate data systems necessary to program administration.[7] Tribal TANF program participants experience barriers to self-sufficiency such as limited employment opportunities and educational attainment and lack of transportation and child care.[8] State-tribal cooperation may facilitate solutions to some of these problems.

There are a number of ways states and tribes may work together to create effective programs for all TANF recipients in the state, whether they are served by a state or tribal program. One example is the allocation of state funding to tribal TANF programs. In addition to helping states meet their MOE requirements, state funding can help tribes further develop and expand their programs, allowing them to better meet the needs of Indian families. This is helpful to the tribal TANF program but also the state, as everyone benefits from increased employment and better outcomes for children and families. In addition, cooperative agreements have been established in some areas to allow the tribal TANF programs to access state data systems to facilitate program administration. Although tribes are permitted to use a portion of their block grant to develop information systems, this would decrease the amount of funding available for direct services to program participants.[9] Cost savings can be realized through intergovernmental agreements that provide for access to the state system, which in turn allows more resources to be dedicated to job readiness and work support services.

Other ways state and tribal policymakers may work together is through efforts to improve data collection and information sharing so that community needs and barriers to employment can be better understood and addressed. Cross-training of program staff can provide opportunities to share best practices and lessons learned. Staff also can be made aware of the requirements associated with both the state and tribal programs. Increased knowledge of each program's requirements and familiarity with program staff can help caseworkers direct clients to the appropriate program and provide more effective services.[10] Finally, overarching efforts to promote infrastructure and economic development can help address lack of employment opportunities for all TANF recipients throughout the state, particularly those residing in rural areas or on isolated reservations.

CHILD SUPPORT ENFORCEMENT

The Child Support Enforcement (CSE) program was established in 1975 under Title IV-D of the Social Security Act as a federal-state partnership.[11] The goal of the program is to ensure that both parents financially support their children. To achieve this goal, CSE programs (also known as IV-D programs) are responsible for locating noncustodial parents, establishing paternity, establishing and enforcing support orders, and collecting support payments from parents who are legally obligated to pay.[12]

Historically state CSE programs have been tasked with carrying out these functions on the reservations, though this was problematic in that states are largely prohibited from exercising jurisdiction over tribal members on tribal land.[13] This situation was improved with the passage of the Personal Responsibility and Work Opportunity Reconciliation Act of

1996. In addition to establishing the TANF program PRWORA authorized direct funding to tribes and tribal organizations to support tribal CSE programs, appropriately aligning federal funding and programmatic authority with tribal civil jurisdictional authority. More than 50 tribes now operate child support programs which provide services to Indian families on tribal land.[14]

It is often difficult to establish and enforce child support orders when the parents reside in two different jurisdictions. The various state or tribal CSE offices can facilitate the establishment and enforcement of such orders, and courts throughout the United States must accord full faith and credit to support orders issued by another state or tribe, provided that court had jurisdiction over the case.[15] State-tribal cooperation can help children being served by a CSE program to get the support they are entitled to. Intergovernmental communication and coordination are helpful whether the tribe is currently operating a CSE program or is considering establishing one. Specifically, states and tribes will want to determine how cross-jurisdictional case processing will be handled, if any intergovernmental agreements exist that govern this process,[16] or if program operations would be facilitated by the development of such agreements.

In addition, a number of other benefits can be derived from state-tribal cooperation on child support issues. Increased communication can provide opportunities to share best practices, identify strategies for program improvement, and identify areas that may benefit from intergovernmental agreements and additional cooperative efforts.

> Collaboration between the Washington Division of Child Support and tribes in the state has resulted in a number of positive outcomes including the establishment of eight tribal CSE programs, agreements with five tribal TANF programs to provide child support services on their tribal TANF cases, agreements with thirteen tribes to provide them with limited access to state computer systems, and more culturally relevant child support services are being provided to both Indian and non-Indian children and families.[17]

Moreover, state-tribal cooperation in Washington has provided for limited wage-holding of tribal employees.[18] Indeed, additional collection remedies can be made possible through cooperative efforts that generally would not be available otherwise (e.g., tribes can provide the state with information on tribal employee wages, per capita payments, trust assets, tribal license revocation, and personal and real property located on the reservation).[19]

EDUCATION PARTNERSHIPS

Upwards of 90 percent of all Native American and Alaska Native elementary and secondary students attend public schools (as opposed to schools operated by the Bureau of Indian Education).[20] Public schools on tribal land are funded by individual states and are subject to state standards and assessments.[21] These schools are typically operated by local school districts and overseen by the state education departments in the states in which they are located. As a result, policymakers have a responsibility to ensure that the state's public schools are meeting the educational needs of Native American and Alaska Native students. Increased collaboration between states and tribes on education is key to this process. The State-Tribal Education Partnership is one such opportunity.

In May 2012 the U.S. Department of Education announced the launch of the State-Tribal Education Partnership (STEP), which is a pilot program that provides funding to support collaboration between tribes and states. These partnerships focus on increasing the role of tribes in the education of Native American and Alaska Native students in the state public school system.[22] The program is open to the tribal education agencies (TEA) of federally recognized or state-recognized tribes (or a consortium of TEAs) in partnership with a state education agency, with a new round of funding awards to be announced in September 2015.[23] An example of past collaborations that have been supported through the STEP program includes a partnership between the Department of Dine Education (DODE) and the New Mexico Public Education Department (NMPED). STEP funds were used to support efforts between the DODE and NMPED focused on developing an effective, culturally relevant professional development program for teachers working with Navajo students and on identifying learning challenges faced by students attending New Mexico public schools located within the Navajo Nation.[24]

Collaborative efforts on education outside of the STEP program are occurring around the nation as well. For example, policymakers within the state legislatures are involved in efforts to provide education on tribal history and culture and to promote knowledge and preservation of Native languages. In Washington legislation was passed during the 2015 legislative session requiring the inclusion of tribal history, culture, treaty rights, and contemporary tribal government and intergovernmental relations in the public school curriculum.[25] School districts will utilize curriculum developed by the Office of the Superintendent of Public Instruction. This resource is provided at no cost, preventing financial burdens on the state's public schools. School districts are required to collaborate with any federally recognized tribes within their districts and with any neighboring tribes to incorporate appropriate information about these tribes into the classroom curriculum and to create classroom and community cultural exchanges. State legislation and collaborative efforts of this nature provide significant educational and social benefits to both Indian and non-Indian students. In addition, this effort holds the potential to promote mutual respect and long-term relationships, potentially benefiting government and a variety of other sectors, as these students are made more knowledgeable about state-tribal relations upon their entry into the workforce.

In Montana legislation was recently passed that provides funding for the establishment of Native language immersion programs within the state school districts encompassing or adjacent to an Indian reservation or in school districts that include schools with an Indian population of more than 10 percent.[26] This legislation was enacted with the goal of raising student achievement, strengthening families, and preserving and perpetuating Indian language and culture. The immersion programs to be supported under this legislation will provide content area instruction to participating students in an Indian language at least 50 percent of the day and will be taught by teachers who are fully proficient in the languages they use for instruction. Many Native languages are in danger of being lost unless efforts are made to preserve them. While "American Indians and Alaska Natives comprise one percent of the total U.S. population, they make up 50 percent of the nation's languages."[27] With the enactment of this legislation, Montana joins Hawaii as the only other state in the United States to date to provide funding for Native language immersion programs. Policymakers in other areas may want to consider similar measures to help restore Native languages and culture and provide an important educational support for Native students in the state public school systems.

BIBLIOGRAPHY/FOR FURTHER READING

1. Newton, Nell Jessup et al., eds., *Cohen's Handbook of Federal Indian Law,* 2012 edition, San Francisco: LexisNexis, 2012.
2. Pevar, Stephen, *The Rights of Indians and Tribes,* New York: Oxford University Press, 2012.
3. Canby Jr., William C., *American Indian Law in a Nutshell,* 5th edition, St. Paul, MN: West Academic Publishing, 2011.
4. Conference of Western Attorneys General, *American Indian Law Deskbook,* 2014 edition, Egan, MN: LegalWorks, 2014.
5. Ashley, Jeffrey S., and Secody J. Hubbard, *Negotiated Sovereignty: Working to Improve Tribal-State Relations,* Westport, CT: Praeger, 2004.
6. Wilkins, David E., *American Indian Politics and the American Political System,* Lanham, MD: Rowman & Littlefield, 2002.
7. Bay, Brad A., and Erin Hogan Fouberg, eds., *The Tribes and the States: Geographies of Intergovernmental Interaction,* Lanham, MD: Rowman & Littlefield, 2002.
8. Atwood, Barbara Ann, *Children, Tribes, and States,* Durham, NC: Carolina Academic Press, 2010.
9. Hanschu, Chantalle, *State-Tribal Consultation Guide: An Introduction for Colorado State Agencies to Conducting Formal Consultations with Federally Recognized American Indian Tribes,* Denver, CO: Colorado Commission of Indian Affairs, 2014.
10. Susan Johnson et al., *Government to Government: Models of Cooperation Between States and Tribes,* Denver, CO: National

Conference of State Legislatures, 2002, updated by Sia Davis, 2009.

11. Fisher, Roger, William Ury, and Bruce Patton, *Getting to Yes: Negotiating Agreement Without Giving In,* New York: Penguin Books, 2011.

12. Chari, Sangitm and Jaime M. N. Lavallee, eds., *Accomplishing NAGPRA: Perspectives on the Intent, Impact, and Future of the Native American Graves Protection and Repatriation Act,* Corvallis: Oregon University Press, 2013.

NOTES

I. BACKGROUND AND INTRODUCTION

1. Tina Norris, Paula L. Vines, and Elizabeth M. Hoeffel, *The American Indian and Alaska Native Population: 2010, 2010 Census Briefs,* U.S. Department of Commerce, Economics and Statistics Administration, U.S. Census Bureau, January 2012, 1.

2. U.S. Department of the Interior, Bureau of Indian Affairs, "Indian Entities Recognized and Eligible to Receive Services from the Bureau of Indian Affairs," *Federal Register* 77, no. 155 (August 10, 2012): 47868. http://www.gpo.gov/fdsys/pkg/FR-2012-08-10/pdf.

3. "Federal and State Recognized Tribes," National Conference of State Legislatures, accessed May 26, 2015, http://www.ncsl.org/research/state-tribal-institute/list-of-federal-and-state-recognized-tribes.aspx#State; "National Caucus of Native American State Legislators," National Conference of State Legislatures, accessed May 26, 2015, http://www.ncsl.org/research/state-tribal-institute/national-caucus-native-american-state-legislators.aspx.

4. Robert J. Miller, *The History of Federal Indian Policies* (Portland, OR: Lewis & Clark Law School, 2010), 2, http://ssrn.com/abstract=1573670.

5. *Johnson v. M'Intosh,* 21 U.S. 543 (1823).

6. *Cherokee Nation v. Georgia,* 30 U.S. 1 (1831).

7. *Worcester v. Georgia,* 31 U.S. 515 (1832).

8. *Seminole Nation v. United States,* 316 U.S. 286, 296–97 (1942).

9. 30 U.S. 1 (1831).

10. 316 U.S. 286 (1942).

11. "Frequently Asked Questions," U. S. Department of the Interior, Indian Affairs, accessed May 26, 2015, http://www.bia.gov/FAQs/.

12. *Seminole* 316 U.S. at 297.

13. "Frequently Asked Questions," U. S. Department of the Interior, Indian Affairs, accessed May 26, 2015, http://www.bia.gov/FAQs/.

14. *Morton v. Mancari*, 417 U.S. 535, 553–54 (1974).

15. Highlights of the Final Federal Acknowledgement Rule (25 CFR 83), Department of Interior, Bureau of Indian Affairs, accessed October 28, 2015, www.bia.gov/cs/groups/public/documents/text/idc1-030769.pdf.

16. Mandatory Criteria for Federal Acknowledgement, Code of Federal Regulations, title 25 U2012): §83.7, http://www/ppo.gov/fdsys/pkg/CFR-2012-title25-vol1-sec83.7.xml.

17. Highlights of the Final Federal Acknowledgement Rule (25 CFR 83), Department of Interior, Bureau of Indian Affairs, accessed October 28, 2015, www.bia.gov/cs/groups/public/documents/text/idc1-030769.pdf; 25 CFR Part 83, Federal Acknowledgement of American Indian Tribes, Executive Summary of Rule, Department of Interior, Bureau of Indian Affairs, accessed October 28, 2015, www.bia.gov/cs/groups/public/documents/text/idc1-030742.pdf.

18. Alexa Koenig and Jonathan Stein, "Federalism and the State Recognition of Native American Tribes: A Survey of State-Recognized Tribes and the State Recognition Process Across the United States," 48 Santa Clara Law Review, 79, 98 (2008).

19. Ibid, 98-99.

20. Miller, *The History of Federal Indian Policies,* 8.

21. Ibid., 7–8.

22. Ibid., 10.

23. Ibid., 11.

24. Ibid., 11–12.

25. Ibid., 12.

26. Ibid.

27. Ibid., 14.

28. Ibid., 15.

29. Ibid.

30. David E. Wilkins, *American Indian Politics and the American Political System* (Lanham, MD: Rowman & Littlefield, 2002), 114.

31. Ibid., 115

32. Ibid., 18

33. Ibid.

34. President Richard Nixon Special Message to the Congress on Indian Affairs on July 8, 1970. Available online at http://www.persidency.ucsb.edu/ws/?pid=2573.

35. Nell Jessup Newton et al., eds., *Cohen's Handbook on Federal Indian Law* (San Francisco, CA: LexisNexis, 2012), 93, citing Thomas Clarkin, *Federal*

Indian Policy in the Kennedy and Johnson Administrations, 1961-1969 (Albuquerque, NM: University of New Mexico Press, 2001); Charles Wilkinson, *Blood Struggle: The Rise of Modern Indian Nations* (W.W. Norton, 2005); *See also* Vine Deloria Jr., ed., *American Indian Policy in the Twentieth Century* (Norman: University of Oklahoma Press, 1985); George Pierre Castile, *To Show Heart: Native American Self-Determination and the Federal Indian Policy, 1960-1975* (Tucson: University of Arizona Press, 1998).

36. Miller, *The History of Federal Indian Policies,* 18.
37. Ibid., 18–19.
38. Stephen Cornell and Jonathan Taylor, "Sovereignty, Devolution, and the Future of Tribal-State Relations" (paper presented at the midyear session of the National Congress of American Indians, Juneau, Alaska, June 26, 2000), 1.
39. Ibid.
40. Ibid., 4.
41. Newton et al., eds., *Cohen's Handbook on Federal Indian Law,* 168.
42. Koenig and Stein, *Federalism and the State Recognition of Native American Tribes,* 83.
43. "Federal and State Recognized Tribes," National Conference of State Legislatures, accessed May 26, 2015, http://www.ncsl.org/research/state-tribal-institute/list-of-federal-and-state-recognized-tribes.aspx#State.
44. Koenig and Stein, *Federalism and the State Recognition of Native American Tribes,* 106–7.
45. Newton et al., eds., *Cohen's Handbook on Federal Indian Law,* 168.
46. Koenig and Stein, *Federalism and the State Recognition of Native American Tribes,* 103–4, 107.
47. Ibid., 103–4.
48. Ibid., 104.
49. Newton et al., eds., *Cohen's Handbook on Federal Indian Law,* 591–92.

2. STATE-TRIBAL CONSULTATION

1. Executive Order 13175 of November 6, 2000, Consultation and Coordination with Indian Tribal Governments, *Code of Federal Regulations,* title 3 (2000): 100–102, http://www.gpo.gov/fdsys/pkg/CFR-2001-title3-vol1/pdf/CFR-2001-title3-vol1-eo13175.pdf.
2. *Memorandum for the Heads of Executive Departments and Agencies: Government-to-Government Relationship with Tribal Governments* in *Public Papers of the Presidents of the United States: George W. Bush, 2001-2009* (Washington, DC: GPO, 2004), 9:23.

3. "Memorandum for the Heads of Executive Departments and Agencies: Tribal Consultation," Presidential Memoranda, White House Office of the Press Secretary, November 5, 2009. Available online at https://www.whitehouse.gov/the-press-office/memorandum-tribal-consultation-signed-president.

4. Ibid.

5. Executive Order 13647 of June 26, 2013, Establishing the White House Council on Native American Affairs, *Code of Federal Regulations,* title 3 (2013): 100–102, http://www.gpo.gov/fdsys/pkg/CFR-2014-title3-vol1/pdf/CFR-2014-title3-vol1-eo13647.pdf.

6. "Centennial Accord between the Federally Recognized Indian Tribes in Washington State and the State of Washington," Governor's Office of Indian Affairs, accessed January 18, 2015, http://www/goia.wa.gov/Government-to-Government/Data/CentennialAccord.htm.

7. "Institutionalizing the Government-to-Government Relationship in Preparation for the New Millennium," Governor's Office of Indian Affairs, accessed January 18, 2015, http://www.goia.wa.gov/Government-to-Government/Data/agreement.htm.

8. Chantalle Hanschu, *State-Tribal Consultation Guide: An Introduction for Colorado State Agencies to Conducting Formal Consultations with Federally Recognized American Indian Tribes* (Denver, CO: Colorado Commission of Indian Affairs, 2014), 9. Available online at https://sandcreekmassacre150.files.wordpress.com/2014/09/co-state-tribal-consultation-guide.pdf.

9. Jeffrey S. Ashley and Secody J. Hubbard, *Negotiated Sovereignty: Working to Improve Tribal-State Relations* (Westport, CT: Praeger Publishers, 2004), 55–56.

10. Ibid., 97.

11. Robert Fisher, William Ury, and Bruce Patton, *Getting to Yes: Negotiating Agreement without Giving In (*New York, NY: Penguin Group, Inc., 2011), xxviii.

12. Ibid., 65.

13. Ibid., 62.

14. Ibid., 33.

15. Ibid., 54–55.

16. Robert V. Wolf, *Widening the Circle: Can Peacemaking Work Outside of Tribal Communities?* (New York: Center for Court Innovation, 2012), 3, http://www.courtinnovation.org/sites/default/files/documents/Widening_Circle.pdf.

17. "Indigenous Peacemaking Initiative," Native American Rights Fund, accessed January 12, 2015, http://www.narf.org/peacemaking/learn_more/index.html.

18. Wolf, *Widening the Circle*, 2, quoting Robert Yazzie, "'Hozho Nahasdlii'—We Are Now in Good Relations: Navajo Restorative Justice," 9 *St. Thomas Law Review* 117 (Fall 1996).

19. Robert V. Wolf, *Peacemaking Today: Highlights of a Roundtable Discussion among Tribal and State Practitioners.* (New York: Center for Court Innovation, 2012), 6–7, http://www.courtinnovation.org/sites/default/files/documents/Peacemaking_Today.pdf.

20. Wolf, *Widening the Circle,* 7.

21. Kauffman & Associates, Inc., *State-Tribal Consultations: A Summary of Best Practices from Washington, Oregon & Minnesota,* submitted to Kitty Marx, Tribal Affairs Group, Center for Medicare and Medicaid Services, Baltimore, MD, August 20, 2013, 3.

22. Ibid., 3.

23. Ibid., 5–6.

24. Kauffman & Associates, Inc., *Best Practices in State-Tribal Consultations: Findings from Oregon,* submitted to Kitty Marx, Tribal Affairs Group, Center for Medicare and Medicaid Services, Baltimore, MD, August 20, 2013, 7–8.

25. Kauffman & Associates, Inc., *Best Practices in State-Tribal Consultations: Findings from Minnesota,* submitted to Kitty Marx, Tribal Affairs Group, Center for Medicare and Medicaid Services, Baltimore, MD, August 20, 2013, 7–8.

3. SOVEREIGN IMMUNITY AND ITS IMPACT ON STATE-TRIBAL RELATIONS

1. *Kiowa Tribe of Oklahoma v. Manufacturing Technologies, Inc.,* 523 U.S. 751, 754 (1998). See also *Three Affiliated Tribes of Fort Berthold Reservations v. Wold Engineering, P.C.,* 476 U.S. 877, 890 (1986); *Santa Clara Pueblo v. Martinez,* 436 U.S. 49, 58 (1978); *United States v. United States Fidelity & Guaranty Co.,* 309 U.S. 506, 512 (1940).

2. Id. at 760.

3. *Santa Clara Pueblo v. Martinez,* 436 U.S. 49, 58 (1978).

4. *Kiowa Tribe of Oklahoma,* 523 U.S. at 754.

5. "An Introduction to Indian Nations in the United States," National Congress of American Indians, accessed March 11, 2015, http://www.ncai.org/about-tribes/indians_101.pdf.

6. *Cogo v. Central Council of Tlingit & Haida Indians,* 465 F. Supp. 1286, 1288 (D. Alaska 1879).

7. Amelia Fogleman, "Sovereign Immunity of Indian Tribes: A Proposal for Statutory Waiver for Tribal Businesses," 79 *Virginia Law Review,* 1345, 1350 (1993), citing *Cogo v. Central Council of the Tlingit and Haida Indians,* 465 F. Supp. 1286, 1288.

8. Ibid., 1347.

9. Fogleman, *Sovereign Immunity of Indian Tribes,* 1373.

10. Gabriel S. Galanda, "Insuring Indian Country," *Insurance Journal,* West Region (May 22, 2006), 140.

11. Ibid.

12. "Topic in Brief: Sovereign Immunity," University of Arizona NativeNet, accessed February 17, 2015, http://www.uanativenet.com/topicitem/Topic%20In%20Brief/97.

13. Galanda, "Insuring Indian Country," 140.

14. John Barrett, Gabriel S. Galanda, Joseph P. Kalt, Lance Morgan, and Robert A. Williams Jr., "Forum on Tribal Sovereign Immunity," University of Arizona NativeNet video (2007), accessed February 17, 2015, http://uanativenet.com/topicitem/Videos/610.

15. Susan Johnson et al., "Government to Government: Models of Cooperation between States and Tribes" (Denver, CO: National Conference of State Legislatures, 2002, updated by Sia Davis, 2009), 63.

16. Gabriel S. Galanda and Anthony S. Broadman, "The Law of Business in Indian Country," *Law Trends & News: Practice Area Newsletter, American Bar Association, General Practice, Solo & Small Firm Division* (Winter 2009), vol. 5, no. 2.

17. Barrett et al., "Forum on Tribal Sovereign Immunity."

18. Ibid.

4. CRIMINAL JURISDICTION

1. *United States v. Wheeler,* 435 U.S. 313, 322–23 (1978).

2. Indian Civil Rights Act, U.S. Code 25 (1968), §1301(2) and (4).

3. General Crimes Act, U.S. Code 25 (1948), §1152.

4. Stephen L. Pevar, *The Rights of Indians and Tribes,* 4th ed. (New York, NY: Oxford University Press, 2012), 129.

5. Major Crimes Act, U.S. Code 25 (1948), §1153(a); William C. Canby Jr., *Canby's American Indian Law in a Nutshell*, 5th ed. (St. Paul, MN: West Publishing Co., 2009), 182.

6. *The Rights of Indians and Tribes,* 129.

7. *The Rights of Indians and Tribes,* 135.

8. *The Rights of Indians and Tribes,* 136.

9. Topic in Brief: Indian Country Crimes Act, University of Arizona NativeNet, accessed March 31, 2015, http://uanativenet.com/topicitem/Topics%20In%20Brief/450. See also *The Rights of Indians and Tribes,* 137.

10. *United States v. McBratney,* 104 U.S. 621, 624 (1881).

11. *Oliphant v. Suquamish Indian Tribe,* 435 U.S. 191, 212 (1978).

12. Pevar, *The Rights of Indians and Tribes,* 145.

13. Arvo Q. Mikkamen, *Indian Country Criminal Jurisdiction Chart,* U.S. Attorney's Office, Western District of Oklahoma, accessed March 31, 2015, http://www.justice.gov/sites/default/files/usao-wdok/legacy/2014/03/25/Indian%20Country%20Criminal%20Jurisdiction%20ChartColor2010.pdf.

14. Pevar, *The Rights of Indians and Tribes,* 147, citing *Mattz v. Arnett,* 412 U.S. 481, 505 (1973); *United States v. Azure,* 801 F.2d 336 (8th Cir. 1986); *United States v. Sohappy,* 770 F.2d 816 (9th Cir. 1985), *cert. denied,* 477 U.S. 906 (1986); *United States v. Burnett,* 777 F.2d 593 (10th Cir. 1985), *cert. denied,* 476 U.S. 1106 (1986).

15. State Jurisdiction Over Offenses Committed by or Against Indians in Indian Country, U.S. Code 18 (1953), §1162(a); Pevar, *The Rights of Indians and Tribes,* 128–29.

16. State Jurisdiction Over Offenses Committed by or Against Indians in Indian Country U.S. Code 18 (1953), §1162(b); Assumption by State of Criminal Jurisdiction, U.S. Code 25 (1968), §1321(b).

17. *The Rights of Indians and Tribes,* 143.

18. *California v. Cabazon Band of Mission Indians,* 480 U.S. 202, 209 (1987); *See also* Pevar, *The Rights of Indians and Tribes,* 114.

19. *California v. Cabazon Band of Mission Indians,* 480 U.S. 202, 209 (1987); *See also* Pevar, *The Rights of Indians and Tribes,* 114.

20. Pevar, *The Rights of Indians and Tribes,* 143, citing *State v. St. Clair,* 560 N.W.2d 732, 734; *State v. Stone,* 572 N.W.2d 725, 729 (Minn. 1997); *State v. Jones,* 729 N.W.2d 1 (Minn. 2007), *cert. denied,* 552 U.S. 1097 (2008).

21. Tribal Law and Order Act of 2010, §202(a)(1) and (4).

22. Tribal Law and Order Act of 2010, §202(a)(7)(3).

23. Pevar, *The Rights of Indians and Tribes,* 133–34.

24. "Violence Against Women Act (VAWA) Reauthorization 201," U.S. Department of Justice, accessed March 31, 2015, http://www.justice.gov/tribal/violence-against-women-act-vawa-reauthorization-2013-0.

25. 435 U.S. 191 (1978).

26. Tribal Law and Order Act of 2010, §202(a)(5)(B) and (C).

27. Topic in Brief: Domestic Violence, University of Arizona NativeNet, accessed March 31, 2015, http://uanativenet.com/topicitem/Topics%20In%20Brief/87.

28. "Violence Against Women Act (VAWA) Reauthorization 2013, U.S. Department of Justice, accessed March 31, 2015, http://www.justice.gov/tribal/violence-against-women-act-vawa-reauthorization-2013-0.

29. Pevar, *The Rights of Indians and Tribes,* 133, citing Carole Goldberg, Duane Champagne, and William D. Falcon, "Combating Crime and Dispensing Justice under P.L. 280," *Indian Country Today*, March 24, 2010 at 5.

30. Pevar, *The Rights of Indians and Tribes,* 133, citing Editorial, "Concurrent Jurisdiction Failures?" *Indian Country Today,* July 14, 2010 at 4.

31. *Children and juvenile code; taking a child into custody; providing notification requirements; effective date,* HB 1834, Oklahoma Legislature, 2015 Regular Session (May 6, 2015), http://webserver1.lsb.state.ok.us/cf_pdf/2015-16%20ENR/hB/HB1834%20ENR.PDF.

32. *Wisconsin Statutes & Annotations,* Agreements on Extradition: Indian Tribes, §976.07, https://docs.legis.wisconsin.gov/statutes/statutes/976/07/2.

33. "The New Mexico Tribal-State Judicial Consortium," Judicial Branch of New Mexico, accessed March 31, 2015, http://tribalstate.nmcourts.gov/.

5. CIVIL JURISDICTION

1. Felix S. Cohen and Rennard Strickland, *Cohen's Handbook on Federal Indian Law* (Charlottesville, VA: Michie, 1982), 270.

2. Nell Jessup Newton et al., eds., *Cohen's Handbook on Federal Indian Law* (San Francisco, CA: LexisNexis, 2012), 505.

3. Ibid., 512.

4. 31 U.S. 515 (1832).

5. Cohen, *Handbook of Federal Indian Law*, 261.

6. Ibid., 267.

7. State Jurisdiction Over Offenses Committed by or Against Indians in Indian Country, U.S. Code 18 (1953), §1162; Stephen L. Pevar, *The Rights of Indians and Tribes*, 4th ed. (New York: Oxford University Press, 2012), 111.

8. Ibid., 155.

9. Cohen, *Handbook of Federal Indian Law*, 350.

10. 450 U.S. 544 (1981).

11. Ibid., 450 U.S. 544, 566.

12. *Atkinson Trading Co., Inc. v. Shirley*, 532 U.S. 645 (2001).

13. *Strate v. A-1 Contractors*, 520 U.S. 438 (1997).

14. *Nevada v. Hicks*, 533 U.S. 353 (2001).

15. *Brendale v. Confed. Yakima Indian Nation*, 492 U.S. 408, 431 (1989); Pevar, *The Rights of Indians and Tribes*, 154.

16. *Plains Commerce Bank v. Long Family Land and Cattle Co.,* 554 U.S. 316, 341 (2008); Pevar, *The Rights of Indians and Tribes*, 154.

17. Pevar, *The Rights of Indians and Tribes,* 154.

18. Ibid., 152, quoting Tex Hall, Kelsey Begay, John Echohawk, and Susan Williams, op-ed., "Tribal Governance and Economic Enhancement Initiative," *Indian Country Today* (October 16, 2002), A5.

19. Ibid., 155.

20. Ibid., 121.

21. 358 U.S. 217 (1959).

22. Pevar, *The Rights of Indians and Tribes*, 124.

23. Ibid., 125.

24. Ibid., 162, citing *State Securities, Inc. v. Anderson,* 506 P.2d 786 (N.M. 1973); *Little Horn State Bank v. Stops,* 555 P.2d 211 (Mont. 1976), *cert. denied,* 431 U.S. 924 (1977); *Bradley v. Deloria,* 587 N.W.2d 591 (S.D. 1998); *Wells v. Wells,* 451 N.W.2d 402, 403 (D.S. 1990); *Francisco v. State,* 556 P.2d 1 (Ariz. 1976); *Martin v. Denver Juvenile Court,* 493 P.2d 1093 (Colo. 1972); *Nevada v. Hicks,* 522 U.S. 353, 356 (2001).

25. Ibid., citing *Executions and Enforcements of Judgments,* 30 Am. Jur 2d §213; *Attachments and Garnishments,* 6 Am. Jur. 2d §25.

26. Ibid., citing *Joe v. Marcum,* 621 F.2d 358 (10th Cir. 1980); *Begay v. Roberts,* 801 P.2d 1111 (Ariz. App. 1991). Contra, *Little Horn State Bank v. Stops,* 555 P.2d 211 (Mont. 1976), *cert. denied,* 431 U.S. 924 (1977).

27. Ibid, citing Nell Jessup Newton et al., eds., *Felix Cohen's Handbook of Federal Indian Law*, 2005 ed., 664–66.

28. Newton et al., *Cohen's Handbook on Federal Indian Law*, 555; Pevar, *The Rights of Indians and Tribes,* 114.

29. Carole Goldberg, *Questions and Answers about Public Law 280*, accessed June 24, 2014, http://www.tribal-institute.org/articles/goldberg/htm.

30. State Jurisdiction Over Offenses Committed by or Against Indians in Indian Country, U.S. Code 18 (1953), §1162(b); Pevar, *The Rights of Indians and Tribes,* 114.

31. Ibid.

32. Ibid., 116.

33. Goldberg, *Questions and Answers about Public Law 280.*

34. Assumption by State of Criminal Jurisdiction, U.S. Code 25 (1968), §§1321–1326.

35. Retrocession of Jurisdiction by State, U.S. Code 25 (1968) §1323(a); Pevar, *The Rights of Indians and Tribes*, 117–18.

36. Duane Champagne and Carole Goldberg, *Captured Justice: Native Nations and Public Law 280* (Durham, NC: Carolina Academic Press, 2012), 12.

37. Ibid., 166.

38. *Indian Tribes—Criminal or Civil Jurisdiction,* Washington Legislature, 2012 Regular Session (June 7, 2012), https://legiscan.com/WA/text/HB2233/2011.

39. Champagne and Goldberg, *Captured Justice: Native Nations and Public Law 280*, 3–4.

40. Ibid., 13.

41. Ibid., 4.

42. Ibid., 158–59.

6. TAXATION

1. Gabriel S. Galanda and Anthony S. Broadman, "The Law of Business in Indian Country," *Law Trends and New Practice Area Newsletter, American Bar Association, General Practice, Solo & Small Firm Division* (Winter 2009), vol. 5, no. 2.

2. Ibid.

3. Stephen L. Pevar, *The Rights of Indians and Tribes*, 4th ed. (New York: Oxford University Press, 2012), 170, citing Rev. Rul. 94-16; Mark J. Cowan, "Leaving Money on the Table(s): An Examination of Federal Income Tax Policy Towards Indian Tribes," 6 *Florida Tax Review* 345, 359 (2004).

4. "An Introduction to Indian Nations in the United States," National Congress of American Indians, accessed April 9, 2015, http://www.ncai.org/about-tribes/indians_101.pdf.

5. *Squire v. Capoeman,* 351 U.S. 1 (1996).

6. Pevar, *The Rights of Indians and Tribes,* 169.

7. *McClanahan v. Arizona Tax Comm'n,* 411 U.S. 164 (1973).

8. *Montana v. Blackfeet Tribe,* 471 U.S. 759, 765 (1985).

9. Pevar, *The Rights of Indians and Tribes*, 170.

10. See *McClanahan v. Arizona Tax Commissioners,* 411 U.S. 164 (1973); *Moe v. Confederated Salish & Kootenai Tribes,* 425 U.S. 463 (1976); *Bryan v. Itasca County, Minnesota,* 426 U.S.373 (1976); *Washington v. Confederated Tribes of Colville Indian Reservation,* 447 U.S. 134, 163 (1980); *Montana v. Blackfeet Tribe,* 471 U.S. 759 (1985); *California v. State Board of Equalization v. Chemehuevi Indian Tribe,* 474 U.S. 9 (1985); *Crow Tribe of Indians v. Montana,* 819 F.2d 895 (9th Cir.1987), *aff'd,* 484 U.S. 997 (1988); *County of Yakima v. Confederated Tribes and Bands of the Yakima Indian Nation,* 502 U.S. 251, 258 (1992); *Oklahoma Tax Commission v. Sac & Fox Nation,* 508 U.S. 114 (1993); *Oklahoma Tax Commission v. Chickasaw Nation,* 515 U.S. 450 (1995); *Cass County, Minnesota v. Leech Lake Band of Chippewa Indians,* 524 U.S. 103 (1998); Pevar, *The Rights of Indians and Tribes,* 170.

11. Pevar, *The Rights of Indians and Tribes,* 171.

12. *Bryan v. Itasca County, Minnesota,* 426 U.S. 373 (1976).

13. *County of Yakima v. Confederated Tribes and Bands of the Yakima Indian Nation,* 502 U.S. 251, 270 (1992).

14. *Washington v. Confederated Tribes of the Colville Indian Reservation,* 447 U.S. 134 (1980).

15. *Atkinson Trading Co. v. Shirley,* 532 U.S. 645, 659 (2001).

16. *Merrion v. Jacarilla Apache Tribe,* 455 U.S. 130 (1982); *Cotton Petroleum Corp. et al. v. New Mexico,* 490 U.S. 163 (1989).

17. *Cotton Petroleum Corp. et al. v. New Mexico,* 490 U.S. 163, 189 (1989).

18. *Washington v. Confederated Tribes of the Colville Indian Reservation,* 447 U.S. 134, 159 (1980).

19. "An Introduction to Indian Nations in the United States," National Congress of American Indians, accessed April 9, 2015, http://www.ncai.org/about-tribes/indians_101.pdf.

20. *Washington v. Confederated Tribes of the Colville Indian Reservation,* 447 U.S. 134, 161–62 (1980); *Oklahoma Tax Comm'n v. Citizen Band Potawatomi Indian Tribe of Oklahoma,* 498 U.S. 505, 514 (1991).

21. *Oklahoma Tax Comm'n v. Citizen Band Potawatomi Indian Tribe of Oklahoma,* 498 U.S. 505, 514 (1991).

22. Judy Zelio, "Piecing Together the State Tribal Tax Puzzle," *States and Tribes: Building New Traditions* (Denver, CO: National Conference of State Legislatures, March 2005), 8.

23. Zelio, "Piecing Together the State Tribal Tax Puzzle," 8, 12.

24. 498 U.S. 505 (1991).

25. Brad A. Bays, "Tribal-State Tobacco Compacts and Motor Fuel Contracts in Oklahoma," in *The Tribes and the States: Geographies of Intergovernmental Cooperation,* Brad A. Bays and Erin Hogan Fouberg, eds. (Lanham, MD: Rowman & Littlefield, 2002), 190.

26. Pevar, *The Rights of Indians and Tribes,* 177, citing "North Dakota, Tribe Reach Accord on Reservation Oil Taxes," *Indian Country Today* (June 11, 2008), at 9.

27. *NM Stat* § 9-11-12.1 (2014); "Tribal Cooperative Agreements," New Mexico Taxation and Revenue Department, accessed May 27, 2015, http://www/tax/newmexico.gov/Governmental/tribal-cooperative-agreements.aspx.

28. Pevar, *The Rights of Indians and Tribes,* 177, citing Wash. Code Ann. §§ 43.06.450-460.

29. Zelio, "Piecing Together the State Tribal Tax Puzzle," 5–6.

30. "Indian Tax Guide," Washington Department of Revenue, accessed April 9, 2015, http://dor.wa.gov/Content/FindTaxesandRates/RetailSalesTax/Indians/IndianTaxGuide/default.aspx.

7. INDIAN GAMING

1. *California v. Cabazon Band of Mission Indians,* 480 U.S. 202 (1987).
2. *Indian Gaming Regulatory Act,* U.S. Code 25 (1988), §2701(4).
3. *Indian Gaming Regulatory Act,* U.S. Code 25 (1988), §2702(1).
4. U.S. Governmental Accountability Office, *Indian Gaming: Preliminary Observations on the Regulation and Oversight of Indian Gaming*, GAO-14-743T (Washington, DC, 2014), introduction, http://www.gao.gov/assets/670/664974.pdf.
5. *Indian Gaming Regulatory Act,* U.S. Code 25 (1988), §2703(6).
6. *Indian Gaming Regulatory Act,* U.S. Code 25 (1988), §2710(a)(1).
7. *Indian Gaming Regulatory Act,* U.S. Code 25 (1988), §2703(7)(A)(i)-(ii).
8. *Indian Gaming Regulatory Act,* U.S. Code 25 (1988), §2710(a)(2).
9. *Indian Gaming Regulatory Act,* U.S. Code 25 (1988), §2710(b)(1)(B).
10. *Indian Gaming Regulatory Act,* U.S. Code 25 (1988), §2703(8).
11. *Indian Gaming Regulatory Act,* U.S. Code 25 (1988), §2710(d)(1)(A)-(C).
12. *Indian Gaming Regulatory Act,* U.S. Code 25 (1988), §2710(b(2)(B)(i)-(v).
13. *Indian Gaming Regulatory Act,* U.S. Code 25 (1988), §2710(d)(3)(A).
14. *Indian Gaming Regulatory Act,* U.S. Code 25 (1988), §2710(d)(3)(D)(i)-(vii).
15. *Indian Gaming Regulatory Act,* U.S. Code 25 (1988), §2710(d)(4).
16. 517 U.S. 44 (1996).
17. Stephen L. Pevar, *The Rights of Indians and Tribes*, 4th ed. (New York: Oxford University Press, 2012), 280, citing 63 Fed. Reg. 3289 (1998).
18. Pevar, *The Rights of Indians and Tribes*, 280, citing *Texas v. United States,* 497 F.3d 491 (5th Cir. 2007), *cert. denied,* 555 U.S. 811 (2008).
19. Pevar, *The Rights of Indians and Tribes*, 280–81.
20. Ibid., 281.
21. *Indian Gaming Regulatory Act,* U.S. Code 25 (1988), §2710(d)(8)(C).
22. *Indian Gaming Regulatory Act,* U.S. Code 25 (1988), §2710(d)(8)(B)(i)-(iii).
23. *Indian Gaming Regulatory Act,* U.S. Code 25 (1988), §2703(4)(A)-(B).
24. *Indian Gaming Regulatory Act,* U.S. Code 25 (1988), §2719(a)(1).
25. *Indian Gaming Regulatory Act,* U.S. Code 25 (1988), §2719(a)(2)(B); Pevar, *The Rights of Indians and Tribes*, 283, noting a separate but fairly similar exception exists for tribes in Oklahoma, see 25 U.S Code (1988), §2719(a)(2)(A).
26. *Indian Gaming Regulatory Act,* U.S. Code 25 (1988), § 2719(b)(1)(i); Pevar, *The Rights of Indians and Tribes*, 284.

27. *Indian Gaming Regulatory Act,* U.S. Code 25 (1988), §2719(b)(1)(ii); Pevar, *The Rights of Indians and Tribes,* 284.

28. *Indian Gaming Regulatory Act,* U.S. Code 25 (1988), §2719(b)(1)(iii); Pevar, *The Rights of Indians and Tribes,* 284.

29. *Indian Gaming Regulatory Act,* U.S. Code 25 (1988), §2719(b)(1)(A); Pevar, *The Rights of Indians and Tribes*, 284.

30. U.S. Government Accountability Office, *Indian Gaming: Preliminary Observations on the Regulation and Oversight of Indian Gaming*, 1, 4.

31. Pevar, *The Rights of Indians and Tribes*, 280.

32. U.S. Government Accountability Office, *Indian Gaming: Preliminary Observations on the Regulation and Oversight of Indian Gaming*, 8.

33. Ibid.

34. Ibid.

35. Ibid.

36. Randall K. Q. Akee and Jonathan B. Taylor, *Social and Economic Change on American Indian Reservations: A Databook of the U.S. Censuses and the American Community Survey, 1990-2010* (Sarasota, FL: The Taylor Policy Group, 2014), 44.

37. Ibid., 13.

38. Ibid., 15.

39. Pevar, *The Rights of Indians and Tribes*, 285, citing Statement of Mark Van Norman, cited in "The Impact of Indian Gaming," *American Indian Report* (April 2005) at 12–13.

40. Randall K. Q. Akee and Jonathan B. Taylor, *Social and Economic Change on American Indian Reservations*, 11, citing S. E. Cornell and J. P. Kalt (1992), *Reloading the Dice: Improving the Chances for Economic Development on American Indian Reservations,* https://nnidatabase.org/db/attachments/text/JOPNAs/2003_CORNELL_kalt_JOPNA_reloadingdice.pdf; M. R. Jorgensen (2000), *Bringing the Background Forward: Evidence from Indian Country on the Social and Cultural Determinants of Economic Development*, Harvard University; R. K. Akee, M. R. Jorgensen, and U. Sunde (2011), *Constitutional Change and Economic Development: Empirical Evidence from American Indian Nations*: 1–37; S. E. Cornell and J. P. Kalt (1994), *Cultural Evolution and Constitutional Public Choice: Institutional Diversity and Economic Performance on American Indian Reservations,* Harvard Project on American Indian Economic Development/John F. Kennedy School of Government; B. C. Vancouver, S. E. Cornell, and J. P. Kalt (1995), "Where Does Economic Development Really Come From? Constitutional Rule among the Contemporary Sioux and Apache," *Economic Inquiry* 33: 402–26; Harvard Project on American Indian Economic Development (2008), *The State of Native Nations: Conditions under U.S. Policies of Self-Determination* (New York: Oxford University Press).

8. ENVIRONMENTAL REGULATION AND NATURAL RESOURCES

1. Steven E. Silvern, "Tribes, States, the EPA, and the Territorial Politics of Environmental Protection," in *The Tribes and the States: Geographies of Intergovernmental Interaction,* Brad A. Bays and Erin Hogan Fouberg, eds. (Lanham, MD: Rowman & Littlefield, 2002), 126.

2. Nell Jessup Newton et al., eds., *Felix Cohen's Handbook of Federal Indian Law* (San Francisco, CA: LexisNexis, 2012), 789.

3. "Indian Policies," American Indian Environmental Office Tribal Portal, U.S. Environmental Protection Agency, accessed April 27, 2015, http://www.epa.gov.tribalportal/basicinfo/presidential-docs.html.

4. "Treatment as State Status," American Indian Environmental Office Tribal Portal, U.S. Environmental Protection Agency, accessed April 27, 2015, http:www.epa.gov/tribalportal/laws/tas.htm.

5. "Roles in Indian Country: Regulatory Requirements," Tribal Compliance Assistance Center, U.S. Environmental Protection Agency, accessed May 28, 2015, http://www.epa.gov/tribalcompliance/rolescountry/riregsdrill.html; Nell Jessup Newton et al., eds., *Felix Cohen's Handbook of Federal Indian Law* 791, citing *Nuclear Waste Policy Act*, 42 U.S. Code (1983), §10101 et. seq.

6. "Treatment as State Status," American Indian Environmental Office Tribal Portal, U.S. Environmental Protection Agency, accessed April 27, 2015, http:www.epa.gov/tribalportal/laws/tas.htm.

7. Newton et al., *Felix Cohen's Handbook of Federal Indian Law*, 793–94.

8. Ibid., 785–86, 789.

9. *Wash. Dep't of Ecology v. EPA*, 752 F.2d 1465 (9th Cir. 1985); Newton et al., *Felix Cohen's Handbook of Federal Indian Law,* 789.

10. *Montana v. United States,* 450 U.S. 544, 565–66 (1981).

11. Bart J. Freedman, Marie E. Quasius, and Alanna E. Peterson, *The Wind River Reservation Treatment-as-State Controversy: How Confusion Undermines Opportunities for Cooperative Governance* (Seattle, WA: K&L Gates, 2014), citing *Brendale v. Confederated Tribes & Bands of Yakima Indian Nation,* 492 U.S. 408, 430–31 (1989). Available online at http://www.klgates.com/the-wind-river-reservation-treatment-as-state-controversy-how-confusion-undermines-opportunities-for-cooperative-governance-06-18-2014/.

12. Provisions for Tribal Criminal Enforcement Authority, *Code of Federal Regulations,* title 40 (1999) §49.8, http://www.gpo.gov/fdsys/granule/CFR-1999-title40-vol1/CFR-1999-title40-vol1-sec49-8; Provisions for Tribal Criminal Enforcement Authority, *Code of Federal Regulations,* title 40 (2013) §123.34, http://www.gpo.gov/fdsys/granule/CFR-2013-title40-vol23/CFR-2013-title40-vol23-sec123-34.

13. "Indian Policies," American Indian Environmental Office Tribal Portal, U.S. Environmental Protection Agency, accessed April 27, 2015, http://www.epa.gov.tribalportal/basicinfo/presidential-docs.html.

14. Susan Johnson et al., *Government to Government: Models of Cooperation Between States and Tribes* (Denver, CO: National Conference of State Legislatures, 2002, updated by Sia Davis, 2009), 66.

15. Ibid.

16. Ibid.

17. "Environmental Commission," Southern Ute Indian Tribe, accessed April 28, 2015, http://www.southernute-nsn.gov/environmental-commission/.

18. *New Mexico v. Mescalero Apache Tribe,* 462 U.S. 324 (1983).

19. *Mescalero Apache Tribe,* 462 U.S. at 342 and 344.

20. *Hunting, Trapping, or Fishing on Indian Land,* U.S. Code 18 (1960), §1165.

21. 450 U.S. 544 (1981).

22. *State jurisdiction over offenses committed by or against Indians in Indian country,* 18 U.S. Code (1953) §1162(b).

23. Pevar, *The Rights of Indians and Tribes,* 193.

24. 391 U.S. 392 (1968).

25. *Puyallup Tribe v. Department of Game of Washington,* 391 U.S. 392, 398 (1968); Pevar, *The Rights of Indians and Tribes,* 193–94.

26. *The Rights of Indians and Tribes,* 199, citing *Puyallup Tribe, Inc. v. Department of Game,* 433 U.S. 165 (1977); *United States v. Michigan,* 653 F.2d 277 (6th Cir. 1981); *United States v. Oregon,* 769 F.2d 1410 (9th Cir. 1985); *Puyallup Tribe, Inc., v. Department of Game,* 391 U.S. 392, 398 (1968); *Minnesota v. Mille Lacs Band of Chippewa Indians,* 526 U.S. 172, 205 (1999); *United States v. Washington,* 384 F. Supp. 312, 342, 402–4 (W.D. Wash. 1974), *aff'd,* 520 F.2d 676 (9th Cir. 1975), *cert. denied,* 423 U.S. 1086 (1976).

27. 207 U.S. 564 (1908).

28. William C. Canby Jr., *American Indian Law in a Nutshell*, 5th ed. (St. Paul, MN: West Academic Publishing, 2011), 473.

29. Ibid., 474.

30. *The Rights of Indians and Tribes,* 208.

31. Ibid.

32. Canby Jr., *American Indian Law in a Nutshell,* 477.

33. Pevar, *The Rights of Indians and Tribes,* 208.

34. Canby Jr., *American Indian Law in a Nutshell*, 490.

35. 373 U.S. 546 (1963).

36. Canby Jr., *American Indian Law in a Nutshell*, 481.

37. Canby Jr., *American Indian Law in a Nutshell*, 483–84.

38. "Landmark Indian Water Rights Settlement Fully Implemented," News Release, U.S. Department of the Interior, March 18, 2008, citing Carl Artman, assistant secretary for Indian Affairs, accessed May 28, 2015, http://www.doi.gov/news/archive/08_News_Releases/080318.html.

39. Canby Jr., *American Indian Law in a Nutshell*, 485.

40. "Reserved Water Rights Compact Commission," Montana Department of Natural Resources and Conservation, accessed April 30, 2015, http://dnrc.mt.gov/divisions/reserved-water-rights-compact–commission.

41. "Compacts with Montana Indian Tribes," Montana Department of Natural Resources and Conservation, accessed April 30, 2015, http://dnrc.mt.gov/divisions/reserved-water-rights-compact-commission/history.

9. NATIVE AMERICAN GRAVES PROTECTION AND REPATRIATION ACT

1. Sangita Chari and Jaime M. N. Lavallee, eds., *Accomplishing NAGPRA: Perspectives on the Intent, Impact, and Future of the Native American Graves Protection and Repatriation Act* (Corvallis: Oregon State University Press, 2013), 8.

2. *Native American Graves Protection and Repatriation Act*, 25 U.S. Code (1990), §3001(8).

3. "National NAGPRA: Frequently Asked Questions," National Park Service, U.S. Department of the Interior, accessed May 14, 2015, http://www.nps.gov/nagpra/FAQ/INDEX/HTM.

4. Ibid.

5. Ibid.

6. Ibid.

7. *At a Glance: 43 CFR 10.11—Disposition of Culturally Unidentifiable Native American Human Remains*, National Park Service, accessed May 14, 2015, http://www.nps.gov/nagpra/DOCUMENTS/At-a-glance-43CFR10.11.pdf; 43 CFR §10.11(b)(1) and (2).

8. Disposition of Culturally Unidentifiable Human Remains *Code of Federal Regulations,* title 43 (2010): §10.11(b)(6), http://www.gpo.gov/fdsys/pkg/CFR-2012-title43-vol1/pdf/CFR-2012-title43-vol1-sec10-11.pdf.

9. *Native American Graves Protection and Repatriation Act*, 25 U.S. Code (1990) §3001(15)(A), (B) and (C).

10. "National NAGPRA: Frequently Asked Questions," National Park Service, U.S. Department of the Interior, accessed May 14, 2015, http://www.nps.gov/nagpra/FAQ/INDEX/HTM.

11. Native American Graves Protection and Repatriation Act, 25 U.S. Code (1990), §3002(a)(1).
12. Native American Graves Protection and Repatriation Act, 25 U.S. Code (1990), §3002(a)(2)(A) and (B).
13. Native American Graves Protection and Repatriation Act, 25 U.S. Code (1990), §3002(a)(2)(C)(1).
14. Native American Graves Protection and Repatriation Act, 25 U.S. Code (1990), §3002(a)(2)(C)(2).
15. "Intentional Excavation on Federal and Tribal Lands after November 16, 1990," National Park Service, accessed May 18, 2015, http://www/nps/gov/nagpra/TRAINING/Intentional_Excavations.pdf.
16. Ibid.
17. Ibid.
18. Ibid.
19. Ibid.
20. "Inadvertent Discoveries on Federal Lands after November 16, 1990," National Park Service, accessed May 18, 2015, http://www.nps.gov/nagpra/TRAINING/Discovery_Fed%20_Lands.pdf.
21. Ibid.
22. Ibid.
23. Ryan M. Seidmann, "What Have the States Done to Expand Human Remains Protections?" *Museum Anthropology* 33 (2010): 203.
24. Ibid., 203, citing Cal. Health & Saf. Code §8011(f).
25. Ibid., 201, citing La. R.S. 8:672.
26. Ibid.
27. Ibid., 202, citing La. R.S. 8:681.
28. Ibid., 202, citing La. R.S. 8:681(4)(c).
29. Bridget Ambler and Sheila Goff, "Implementing NAGPRA at History Colorado: Applying Cultural Property Legacy Collections and Forging Tribal Parternships," in *Accomplishing NAGPRA: Perspectives on the Intent, Impact, and Future of the Native American Graves Protection and Repatriation Act*, eds. Sangita Chari and Jaime M. N. Lavallee (Corvallis: Oregon State University Press, 2013), 205.
30. Ibid., 206.
31. Ibid., 207.
32. Ibid., 211.
33. Ibid., 212.
34. Ibid., 216.
35. Ibid., 211.
36. Ibid., 198.

10. THE INDIAN CHILD WELFARE ACT

1. *Indian Child Welfare Act,* U.S. Code 25 (1978) §1901(2) and (3).

2. U.S. Congress, House of Representatives, *Establishing Standards for the Placement of Indian Children in Foster or Adoptive Homes to Prevent the Break-up of Indian Families and for Other Purposes (Report to accompany H.R. 12533)*, 95th Cong., 2d sess., 1978, H.Rep. 1386, 10.

3. Ibid., 9.

4. "Assistant Secretary Washburn Announces Revised Guidelines to Ensure that Native Children and Families Receive the Full Protection of the Indian Child Welfare Act," News Release, Office of the Assistant Secretary, U.S. Department of the Interior, February 24, 2015, accessed March 17, 2015, http://www.bia.gov/cs/groups/public/documents/text/idc1-029449.pdf.

5. *Indian Child Welfare Act,* U.S. Code 25 (1978) §1902.

6. Department of the Interior, Bureau of Indian Affairs, "Guidelines for State Courts and Agencies in Indian Child Custody Proceedings," *Federal Register* 80, no. 37 (February 25, 2015): 10146, Section B.3.(d). http://www.gpo.gov/fdsys/pkg/FR-2015-02-25/html/2015-03925.htm.

7. *Indian Child Welfare Act,* U.S. Code 25 (1978), §1911(a).

8. *Indian Child Welfare Act,* U.S. Code 25 (1978), §1911(d).

9. *Indian Child Welfare Act,* U.S. Code 25 (1978), §1911 (b) and (c).

10. *Indian Child Welfare Act,* U.S. Code 25 (1978), §1922(e).

11. *Mississippi Choctaw Indian Band* v. *Holyfield,* 490 U.S. 30, 46–47 (1989).

12. Ibid., 48–49.

13. *Indian Child Welfare Act,* U.S. Code 25 (1978), §1912(a).

14. Department of Interior, Bureau of Indian Affairs, "Guidelines for State Courts and Agencies in Indian Child Custody Proceedings," *Federal Register* 80, no. 37 (February 25, 2015): 10146, Section A.3.(d). http://www.gpo.gov/fdsys/pkg/FR-2015-02-25/html/2015-03925.htm.

15. *Indian Child Welfare Act,* U.S. Code 25 (1978), §1912(e).

16. *Indian Child Welfare Act,* U.S. Code 25 (1978), §1912(f).

17. *Indian Child Welfare Act,* U.S. Code 25 (1978), §1915(b).

18. *Indian Child Welfare Act,* U.S. Code 25 (1978), §1915(a).

19. Department of the Interior, Bureau of Indian Affairs, "Guidelines for State Courts and Agencies in Indian Child Custody Proceedings," *Federal Register* 80, no. 37 (February 25, 2015): 10146, Section F.1(a). http://www.gpo.gov/fdsys/pkg/FR-2015-02-25/html/2015-03925.htm.

20. *Indian Child Welfare Act,* U.S. Code 25 (1978), §1918(a).

21. *Indian Child Welfare Act,* U.S. Code 25 (1978), §1919(a).

22. Department of the Interior, Bureau of Indian Affairs, "Guidelines for State Courts and Agencies in Indian Child Custody Proceedings," *Federal Register* 80, no. 37 (February 25, 2015): 10146, Section A.5.(b). http://www.gpo.gov/fdsys/pkg/FR-2015-02-25/html/2015-03925.htm.

23. Department of the Interior, Bureau of Indian Affairs, "Guidelines for State Courts and Agencies in Indian Child Custody Proceedings," *Federal Register* 80, no. 37 (February 25, 2015) 10146. http://www.gpo.gov/fdsys/pkg/FR-2015-02-25/html/2015-03925.htm.

24. Department of the Interior, Bureau of Indian Affairs, "Guidelines for State Courts and Agencies in Indian Child Custody Proceedings," *Federal Register* 80, no. 37 (February 25, 2015): 10146, Section A.2.(1)-(15). http://www.gpo.gov/fdsys/pkg/FR-2015-02-25/html/2015-03925.htm.

25. Department of the Interior, Bureau of Indian Affairs, "Guidelines for State Courts and Agencies in Indian Child Custody Proceedings," *Federal Register* 80, no. 37 (February 25, 2015): 10146, Section F.4.(a)-(c). http://www.gpo.gov/fdsys/pkg/FR-2015-02-25/html/2015-03925.htm.

26. Department of the Interior, Bureau of Indian Affairs, "Guidelines for State Courts and Agencies in Indian Child Custody Proceedings," *Federal Register* 80, no. 37 (February 25, 2015): 10146, Section C.3.(a) and (c). http://www.gpo.gov/fdsys/pkg/FR-2015-02-25/html/2015-03925.htm.

27. Department of the Interior, Bureau of Indian Affairs, "Guidelines for State Courts and Agencies in Indian Child Custody Proceedings," *Federal Register* 80, no. 37 (February 25, 2015): 10146, Section D.3.(a) and (b). http://www.gpo.gov/fdsys/pkg/FR-2015-02-25/html/2015-03925.htm.

28. Department of the Interior, Bureau of Indian Affairs, "Guidelines for State Courts and Agencies in Indian Child Custody Proceedings.," *Federal Register* 80, no. 37 (February 25, 2015): 10146, Section D.4.(a) and (b). http://www.gpo.gov/fdsys/pkg/FR-2015-02-25/html/2015-03925.htm.

29. Barbara Ann Atwood, *Children, Tribes, and States: Adoption and Custody Conflicts over American Indian Children* (Durham, NC: Carolina Academic Press, 2010), 199.

30. *Adoptive Couple v. Baby Girl,* 133 S.Ct. 2552 (2013). In this case the birth father's tribal membership was not immediately confirmed and timely notice of the child's adoption was not provided to the birth father or the child's tribe, as required by ICWA. The child spent 27 months in the care of a non-Indian couple who had petitioned to adopt the child. The court ruled that key provisions of ICWA that likely would have changed the child's placement from the non-Indian couple to the birth father did not apply.

31. "Assistant Secretary Washburn Announces Revised Guidelines to Ensure that Native Children and Families Receive the Full Protection of the Indian Child Welfare Act," News Release, Office of the Secretary, U.S. Department of the

Interior, February 24, 2015, accessed March 17, 2015, http://www.bia.gov/cs/groups/public/documents/text/idc1-029449.pdf.

32. *Indian Child Welfare Act,* U.S. Code 25 (1978), §1931(a).

33. Barbara Ann Atwood, *Children, Tribes, and States: Adoption and Custody Conflicts over American Indian Children* (Durham, NC: Carolina Academic Press, 2010), 199.

34. Ibid.

35. "Tribal Access to Title IV-E Funding Through Direct Federal Access," National Child Welfare Resource Center for Tribes, A Service of the Children's Bureau, Office of the Administration for Children and Families, accessed March 17, 2015, http://www.nrc4tribes.org/Direct-Tribal-Title-IV-E-Funding.cfm.

11. HUMAN SERVICES

1. "Tribal TANF," Office of Family Assistance, Office of the Administration for Children and Families, accessed May 8, 2015, http://www.acf.hhs.gov/programs/tribal/tribal-tanf.

2. Ibid.

3. Ibid.

4. U.S. Government Accountability Office, *Temporary Assistance to Needy Families: HHS Needs to Improve Guidance and Monitoring of Tribal Programs,* GAO-11-758 (Washington, DC, 2011), 8, http://www.gao.gov/assets/590/585311.pdf.

5. Ibid., 7.

6. Ibid.

7. Ibid., 24.

8. Ibid., 24, 28.

9. Ibid., 28.

10. Andrea Wilkins, "Welfare Reform on Tribal Lands: Examples of State-Tribal Collaboration," *States and Tribes: Building New Traditions* (Denver, CO: National Conference of State Legislatures, February 2004), 6.

11. "Building a Tribal IV-D Program: A Guide to the Start-Up Application Process," Administration for Children and Families, accessed May 8, 2015, 1, http://wwwacf.hhs.gov/sites/dafault/files/ocse/im_05_06a.pdf.

12. Ibid.

13. Ibid.

14. "Tribal Agencies," Office of Child Support Enforcement, Office of the Administration for Children and Families, accessed May 8, 2015, http://www/acf/hhs/gov/programs/css/tribal-agencies.

15. "Handbook on Child Support Enforcement: Answers to Your Questions," Department of Health and Human Services, Administration for Children and Families, Office of Child Support Enforcement, accessed May 8, 2015, http://publications.usa.gov/epublications/childrenf/interstate.htm#state.

16. "Building a Tribal IV-D Program: A Guide to the Start-Up Application Process," 15.

17. "State/Tribal Partnerships in Washington State," Department of Social and Health Services, Division of Child Support Tribal Relations Team, accessed May 8, 2015, https://www.dshs.wa.gov/sites/default/files/ESA/dcs/documents/TribalChildSupportPartnerships.pdf.

18. Ibid.

19. Ibid.

20. "Native Education 101: Basic Facts about American Indian, Alaska Native, and Native Hawaiian Education," National Indian Education Association, accessed May 8, 2015, 3, http://niea.org/data/files/policy/nativeeducation101.pdf.

21. Ibid., 10.

22. State Tribal Education Partnership (STEP), U.S. Department of Education, accessed May 8, 2015, http://www2.ed.gov/programs/step/index.html?exp=0.

23. Ibid.

24. State Tribal Education Partnership (STEP) Awards, U.S. Department of Education, accessed May 8, 2015, http://www2.ed.gov/programs/step/awards.html.

25. *An Act Relating to Teaching Washington's Tribal History, Culture, and Government in the Common Schools,* Substitute SB 5433, Washington Legislature, 2015 Regular Session (May 8, 2015), http://lawfilesext.leg.wa.gov/biennium/2015-16/Pdf/Bills/Senate%20Passed%20Legislature/5433-S.PL.pdf.

26. *Cultural Integrity Commitment Act,* SB 0272, Montana Legislature, 2015 Regular Session (May 6, 2015), http://leg.mt.gov/bills/2015/sb0299/SB0272_x.pdf.

27. "Native Education 101: Basic Facts about American Indian, Alaska Native, and Native Hawaiian Education," National Indian Education Association, accessed May 8, 2015, 8, http://niea.org/data/files/policy/nativeeducation101.pdf.

INDEX

www.ingramcontent.com/pod-product-compliance
Ingram Content Group UK Ltd.
Pitfield, Milton Keynes, MK11 3LW, UK
UKHW040418181125
465134UK00003BA/455

9 781442 251403